The Legacy of the Second World War

BOOKS BY JOHN LUKACS

The Great Powers and Eastern Europe

Tocqueville: The European Revolution
and Correspondence with Gobineau (editor)

A History of the Cold War

Decline and Rise of Europe

A New History of the Cold War

Historical Consciousness; or, The Remembered Past

The Passing of the Modern Age

A Sketch of the History of Chestnut Hill College, 1924–1974

The Last European War: September 1939–December 1941

1945: Year Zero

Philadelphia, Patricians, and Philistines, 1900–1950

Outgrowing Democracy: A History of the
United States in the Twentieth Century

Budapest 1900: A Historical Portrait of a
City and Its Culture

Confessions of an Original Sinner

The Duel: The Eighty-Day
Struggle Between Churchill and Hitler

The End of the Twentieth Century and the End of the Modern Age

Destinations Past: Traveling through History with John Lukacs

George F. Kennan and the Origins of Containment,
1944–1946: The Kennan-Lukacs Correspondence

The Hitler of History

A Thread of Years

Five Days in London: May 1940

A Student's Guide to the Study of History

At the End of an Age

Churchill: Visionary. Statesman. Historian.

A New Republic: A History of the United States in the Twentieth Century

Democracy and Populism: Fear and Hatred

Remembered Past: John Lukacs on History,
Historians, and Historical Knowledge

June 1941: Hitler and Stalin

George Kennan: A Study of Character

Blood, Toil, Tears, and Sweat: The Dire Warning,
Churchill's First Speech as Prime Minister

Last Rites

JOHN LUKACS

The Legacy of the Second World War

Yale University Press ◆ New Haven and London

Set in Galliard type by Keystone Typesetting, Inc., Orwigsburg, Pennsylvania. Printed in the United States of America.

ISBN 978-0-300-11439-3 (cloth : alk. paper)
Library of Congress Control Number: 2008942446

A catalogue record for this book is available from the British Library.

This paper meets the requirements of ANSI/NISO Z39.48-1992 (Permanence of Paper).

10   9   8   7   6   5   4   3   2

Contents

Contents

Seventy Years Later: The Legacy of the Second World War

This is not a history *of* the Second World War but a book *about* its history. It was written and it will be published about seventy years after the Second World War began, and more than sixty years after it ended. The Second World War was the last of world wars, and with it ended an entire age of history — I shall attempt to argue that a few pages anon, in Chapter 2. One, but only one, reason for this book is that interest in the Second World War goes on and on, more enduring than interest in the First (even though the First World War had led to the Second, and the origins and causes of the First are still discussed by historians here and there). This interest is evident, among other things, in the number of television programs and movies confected about the Second World War and in the large readership of books, journals, articles, and even plays relating to it.

What are the reasons for this persistent popular interest in events of the Second World War even now, two or three generations afterward? One element of this curiosity is, I think, that many events of the Second World War were more dramatic than those of the First. Another element is the lamentable human inclination to be fascinated with what is horrible, with acts, records, memories of brutalities: that therefore many people see something in the Second World War as if it had been a War against Evil — which is its simplified categorization. None of the wars and civil wars since 1945 inspire anything like this interest in the Second World War. Moreover: it is possible, even probable, that the structure of international (and even political) history may have irrevocably changed since then — something worth thinking about, even though the subject of this book is history, not prophecy.

Let me add that I lived most of the formative years of my youth during the years 1939 to 1945, and in the middle of Europe, whence my interest in their history and in its problems. Yet of my books not more than one out of every four dealt with topics of the Second World War. Still, I have been thinking and here and there writing about it during much of my life and career — it is, after all, one of my main interests. But another, more important, concern of mine is the very nature of history, of the problems of its consciousness and of our knowledge of it. These two concerns are inseparable, at least in my mind. There is a difference between history and law; and between their evidences; and even between their purposes. Law, in most civilized nations, does not permit multiple jeopardy: an accused person may be tried only once. But history consists of an endless reconsideration of men and events of the past — moreover: of evidences of their acts but also of their thinking: evidences permissible in history but not in law. That is due not only to the rediscovery of "new" evidences — for history does not only consist of documents, it is not only the recorded but also the remembered past. It is also due to the unavoidable condition that we see the past from a forever moving and changing present. And there is the difference between the purpose of law and the purpose of history. The purpose of law is the establishment of justice and the elimination of injustice. The purpose of history is the pursuit of truth through eliminating untruths. Allow me to relate this to our general knowledge and estimation of the Second World War. There are still many untruths current about the Second World War.

At least in Western Europe, Britain, America, Russia, people consider it having been a war that necessarily had to be fought. There is a general consensus among these peoples that the Second World War was A Good War. (That very phrase "A Good War," as well as "The Greatest Generation," appeared in the United States some time after the 1960s, at least to some extent consequent to the popular unease with the Vietnam War and in contrast to that military struggle.) But there were (and still are) peoples — including later generations — who did not and do not see the Second World War and its outcome as "good." Most of these people and their descendants were on the losing side of the Second World War. They include many of the peoples of Central and Eastern Europe. There is, too, Japan, where as late as 2006 the prime minister chose to pay tribute at the memorial honoring the nation's leaders during the Second World War, including men who had been condemned as instigators of that war or as war criminals. That is regrettable: but — at least in some ways — understandable.

There is another, related, matter. It is amazing how many national, political, ideological inclinations still hark back to the

Second World War.* Many political and ideological divisions in many nations — including nations that did not end up as losers in 1945 — divisions even now, more than sixty years later, relate to the Second World War. They are, at times, represented by political parties. We may — though not always, and not accurately — ascertain their popular appeal from the percentages of their votes. Here is one example. The postwar establishment of the independence of the state of Austria and the subsequent prosperity its people were due to the western Allies' victory in 1945. Yet at least one quarter of the Austrian people, dissatisfied with the sometimes uninspiring and at times corrupting monopoly of their two political parties, have a positive view of many of the accomplishments and memories of the Third Reich, regretting implicitly — and sometimes even explicitly — its defeat and disappearance.† In Italy neo-Fascist parties get about 12 percent of the national vote.‡ In France, six decades after its liberation, Jean-Marie Le Pen's National Front was able to gather 18 percent in 2002.§ Without exception, the ideas of these so-called right-wing

---

* One example of this is the inseparability of Zionism from the cultivation of the memories of the Holocaust, an understandable inclination: yet these two concerns were not entirely identical during the Second World War (consider only that the very word *Holocaust* did not appear and become common until the late 1960s).

† Jörg Haider, leader of a third, nationalist Austrian party, who collected nearly 30 percent of Austrian votes in 2003, on at least one occasion declared Winston Churchill to have been "a war criminal." (In 1943 it was Churchill who, at the Teheran Conference, insisted on and succeeded in declaring the independence of Austria a common aim of the wartime alliance.)

‡ Mussolini's body, secretly recovered by some of his followers, now rests in a kind of mausoleum at his birthplace, Predappio, visited every day by throngs of his admirers, who bring flowers and inscriptions in his honor. About the decoration of Hitler's parents' grave see pages 88–89.

§ The main appeal of Le Pen's party (and also of nationalist parties elsewhere in Europe) is its understandable opposition to the accumulation of (more precisely: radically nationalist) parties rest on their views of the Second World War, views contrary to the accepted views of their governments and of other governments.*

In the United States, too, there were, and still are, people who did or do not think that the Second World War was a Good War. I am not referring to the customary small minority of idealist pacifists but to people who, on occasion, thought and said and wrote that America's alliance with the Soviet Union — and, more telling: its support of Churchill's Britain in 1940 and 1941 — was wrong. At that time this was an "isolationist" (in reality, rather a nationalist and populist) minority, even though a considerable one, represented by such national figures as the ex-president Herbert Hoover, Senator Robert Taft, and the national hero Charles Lindbergh. But soon after the Second World War they and their supporters became the core of the American "conservative" movement — worth noting, since three decades later "conservatives" became something like a majority among the American people, electing popular Republican presidents, of a party that had be-

---

immigrants. But on innumerable occasions Le Pen has stated that the German occupation of France during the Second World War was not a national tragedy. Among other things he has extolled as a French national martyr and hero Robert Brasillach — an extreme Nazified French intellectual, one of the few condemned to death in 1945 whom General De Gaulle refused to pardon.
* In Germany extreme nationalist parties whose essential ideology rests on a positive appreciation of the former Third Reich receive at most 5 to 9 percent of votes; but does this mean that 95 or 91 percent of the German people (whether in the 1950s or in the 1970s or in the 2000s) have had nothing but contempt for their national history during the Second World War? We cannot tell. And now that International Communism is just about dead, it is noteworthy that something like a Nationalist International (*not* an oxymoron) does exist. Its parties and associations sympathize with and support one another; their publications regularly print items about other right-wing nationalist parties in other countries.

come nationalist and populist. It is true that by now not many American "conservatives" suggest or say that the Second World War was not a good cause; but some of them still do.*

No war is truly a Good War. It is only that the aims of one war may be better than those of another war. In this book I shall have to return, again and again, to the recognition that the Second World War was a gigantic global struggle between, by and large, three forces: Western and parliamentary democracy, represented and incarnated by the English-speaking peoples of the world and by other nations of Western Europe; Communism, represented and incarnated by the Soviet Union; and National Socialism, represented and incarnated by the German Third Reich.† And the power of the last, stunningly, was such that it took an alliance of the three, America, Russia, and the British Empire, to defeat it: *no one or even two of them sufficed* to conquer Hitler's Germany.‡ However: in the Pacific, American power sufficed to defeat Japan.

◆ ◆ ◆

Somewhere, in the middle heart of Europe, in the black shadows of the Alpine mountains, in a small town along a quick-flowing cold river, amid a gnarled and dark-browed people, with their minds less and less dependent on the tattered shroud of their Catholic religion or on their sense of loyalty to a once old-German

*One example: a book by Patrick Buchanan (once a confidant of and speechwriter for Ronald Reagan), excoriating Churchill and stating that the entire Second World War against Hitler's Germany had been a mistake—on a best-seller list in 2008.

†To these we may add a few authoritarian (not totalitarian) regimes, opposed to Communism but also to Germany and Japan; to wit, Portugal, Greece, China, and others.

‡In July 1941 in Moscow, Stalin told Harry Hopkins, Roosevelt's confidant, that America *must* enter the war, because Germany's power was such that the Russian and the British empires together could not defeat it.

but now tattered multinational monarchy, a lonely sullen boy came into this world, his heart bitten with rage and ambition, desperately alone as he grew more and more conscious of his destiny of being a German. And then discovering — relatively late, in his thirtieth year — that his bitterness and rage and hate were there in the hearts and minds of thousands of other people around him, too; that God (*a* God of history? or *the* God of Germandom?) had given him a power to speak, a talent to touch their minds and hearts, for the sake of something large and hard. And then this odd and uneasy young man, surer of his ideas than of himself, became the solitary leader of a small party. And then of a larger party. And then of a veritable movement. And then of the largest national party athwart Germany. By then he was convinced that he could — democratically, legally, and inevitably — step over all obstacles to become the chancellor of Germany. And then, when he was the unquestioned and unquestionable head of a great nation, largely united behind him, his Germany would become the strongest and greatest power in Europe, as he subdued and silenced each of his opponents, older men of an older world. And then, if necessary, forced his will on them through wars that he and his Germans must win and would go on winning. Ah! he was not one fortunate person riding atop a great wave; he was more than the figurehead of a nation; more even than a standard dictator. A strange phenomenon, breaking through myth and mist on occasion with hoarse cries, unfathomable by many of his enemies, matching them with the force of his hatreds, with his instincts that were powerful enough to make him a master of war and even a statesman of a kind, on occasion. And thus he and his Germans withstood the greatest empires of the world, the British and the Russian and the American empires, perhaps as many as five hundred million people ranged against a Germany of eighty million — until the very end, here and there even for a few days and nights after his immolation of himself under the ruins of his capital city Berlin.

He alone began the Second World War. It also ended with him. Not only in Europe. Had he not conquered Western Europe there would have been no Japanese thrust against the French and Dutch in the Far East, had there been no Atlantic war between Germany and Britain there would have been no Pacific war of Japan against the British Empire and the United States, surely not in 1941. Four years later the defeat of Japan was inevitably consequent to the disappearance of its great German ally. The Second World War was Hitler's war.

◆ ◆ ◆

And now I must proceed to a dismissal: to a dismissal of a widespread and untruthful view of the twentieth century (historically speaking a brief century, seventy-five years long, 1914 to 1989). This is the belief that this century was marked by the struggle of Democracy against Communism (or of "Freedom" against "Totalitarianism"). If so, then the Second World War, the war against Hitler's National Socialist Germany, was but an unnatural episode, interrupting the greater "epic" confrontation of Democracy against Communism.

What nonsense this is. The two great world wars were the two mountain ranges that dominated the entire history of the twentieth century. Communist rule in Russia was a result (and only one of the results) of the First World War. The so-called cold war between Democracy and Communism (more precisely: between the United States and the Soviet Union) was a consequence of the Second World War, of Hitler's war. (So was the dissolution of the great colonial empires, of the British, French, and Dutch, a consequence of the two world wars.) And then, hardly more than forty years after Russia's victory in 1945, the Soviet empire fell apart, one Communist government disappearing after another, the Russian empire reduced to a size smaller than it had been more than three hundred years ago. Had Hitler's Germany won the war in 1940 or 1941 (and it came very close to that), there is no reason to believe that the Third Reich, that Germany's empire, would have collapsed by 1989 (exactly one hundred years after Adolf Hitler was born).

Consider something else, too: that comparing the quantity of Stalin's or Mao Tse-tung's victims with that of Hitler's results in a, necessarily imprecise, list of numbers — and it tells us nothing. Germany was in the heart, in the center, part and parcel of European and Western civilization, culture, traditions. Russia (and of course China) were not. Stalin had a predecessor, Ivan the Terrible. Hitler had none. His and German National Socialist brutality were unprecedented. Russian brutality was not.

◆ ◆ ◆

Seventy years later we must understand, too, that Germany and National Socialism represented an intellectual and spiritual and ideological movement that for a while — throughout the 1930s and at least during the first part of the Second World War — was very powerful, surely in Europe. By and large this was a reaction against Communism and, perhaps even more, against international capitalism, and against the liberal and democratic intellectual ideas and political practices of the nineteenth century that, from many angles of views, seemed antiquated and corrupt by the 1930s at latest.* Here is a brief (and necessarily imperfect)

---

* We must be careful with these words. A reaction, yes; but reactionary this

list of important, or at least significant writers, thinkers, artists whose contempt for the liberal order or disorder (including, in many cases, their anti-Semitism) was such that they, on occasion, identified themselves with Hitler's (or often with Mussolini's) ideas, some of them sacrificing their careers and even lives beyond the very end: the great Norwegian writer Knut Hamsun; the American Ezra Pound; in France, Louis-Ferdinand Céline, Drieu la Rochelle, Henry de Montherlant; in Germany, Gerhard Hauptmann, Carl Schmitt, Martin Heidegger, Ernst Jünger (the last two at least for a while); the Englishman Wyndham Lewis; Giovanni Papini in Italy; and many less-well-known figures, especially in Central and Eastern Europe, many kinds of Austrian, Slovak, Croatian, Hungarian, Rumanian, and other writers and poets. Above and beyond them, on a higher level, take a glimpse at two, perhaps greatest and deepest, European thinkers and writers of that time: the Spanish José Ortega y Gasset, who chose to live in self-imposed exile in Argentina in 1939, and the French Catholic Georges Bernanos, a towering figure of Free France, who chose his self-imposed exile in Brazil in 1938. (Each returned to his native country before his death, after the war.) Both

---

inclination was not. The mistake of many conservatives across Europe (and especially and disastrously of German conservatives such as Papen and others) was their belief that the great change, including Hitler, was a natural swinging of the pendulum of history backward, away from the ideas and principles of 1789, of the French Revolution. They—like, alas, many "conservative" thinkers even now—did not see, or did not wish to see, that Hitler and National Socialism were populist and modern (and even democratic, in the narrow sense of that word, extolling popular sovereignty). Hitler's contempt for the old and creaking aristocratic and monarchical states of the eighteenth century was deeper and stronger than his dismissal of 1789. (Carlyle, whom Hitler admired, would, had he lived into the twentieth century, unquestionably have admired Hitler. Burke, who saw 1789 otherwise than did Carlyle, would have not.)

kept largely silent about the stunning phenomenon of Hitler, throughout and even after the war. In the nine large volumes of Ortega's collected works (*Obras completas*) there is but one mention of Hitler ("a hypernationalist"). In his rare mentions of Hitler, Bernanos, this profound French patriot and prophetic seer, apostle of resistance against Germany, wrote about Hitler: his rages rose from the depths of the tortured mind of a deeply "humiliated child."

◆ ◆ ◆

In 1945 the defeat of Hitler and of his Germany was complete; and, except for a small number of embittered ideological fanatics his movement did not survive the war. Yet one of his important convictions lives on. This was his recognition that a nation is more important than a state.* I will argue in Chapter 4 that he was an extreme nationalist even more than a racist; and that, even though often he had to consider the interests of the German state not only above the interests of National Socialist ideology but also above those of German nationality, he believed and, on occasion, said that the state is a framework dictated by necessity, while the essence of history is the nation, *Volk*, whose existence both precedes and survives that of states. Now consider that nationalism — a populist phenomenon, and therefore distinguishable from an old-fashioned patriotism† — is still the principal political factor even now, seventy years later, in many places of the world, including even the United States. Consider, too, that less than six months after Hitler's disappearance and defeat

---

*This is one reason why the word *totalitarian,* meaning the total police rule of a state, is incorrect. Another reason: the rule of everyday life, even in Hitler's Germany or in Stalin's Russia, was never "total" or complete.
†Nationalism is the illegitimate marriage of patriotism with a habitual inferiority complex.

Juan Perón in Argentina came to power as the leader of a new nationalist and socialist and populist movement: a minor example, but an example nonetheless.

At that time, too, Stalin's Russian nationalism had become more and more evident. Here is a major example of the superior timeliness of nationalism over internationalism, or of National Socialism over Communism. Some time in the 1930s Stalin — entirely contrary to Marx and to Lenin — recognized the importance of the state over an internationalist ideology. There are myriad evidences of this. In this case — as also in others — Stalin's nationalism followed Hitler's. And then, during the war, his rhetoric of a nationalist patriotism, his restoration of the prestige and of some of the powers of the Russian Orthodox Church, his evocation of historic tsarist generals and other precedents were the results not of calculations but of his genuine inclinations. He would propagate and support Communism and Communists abroad, especially in the portion of Europe that fell under his sway: but employing them as secondary instruments of his statesmanship — ultimately to the Soviet Union's demise. For it was nationalism, much more than economic malfunctionings, or than the almost complete disappearance of the attractions of an internationalist ideology, that brought about the end of Stalin's once great Russian-dominated empire in 1989 — which year was, as I wrote earlier, the end of the cold war *and* the end of the twentieth century, exactly one hundred years after Hitler was born.

At least in the Western world there are few people who choose to openly rehabilitate Hitler. Even those who respect or admire the Third Reich and National Socialism find it best to attack Hitler's Second World War opponents rather than openly extol him. We have also seen that the portion of voters who in some countries reject liberalism or parliamentary democracy amounts

to about 15 percent — if such electoral statistics are clear indica-
tions of national sentiments, which they are not. What we ought
to recognize is that most, if not all, of these political and ideological preferences are rooted in what people, even now, keep thinking about the Second World War.

◆ ◆ ◆

In a way — but only in a way — I will in the following six chapters
attempt to answer six questions. Was the Second World War
inevitable? Was the division of Europe inevitable? Was Hitler
inevitable? Was the making of atomic bombs inevitable? Was
America's war against Germany inevitable? Was the cold war
inevitable? I must pursue — even though briefly — the meaning of
"inevitability" for the historian.* Again, in a way — but only in a
way — nothing in the history of a man, or of a nation, or of a war,
or of an entire civilization, is inevitable. But then, in a more
mundane sense, this leads us to the sometimes posed question:
"What if?" Recently some historians have been occupying themselves with speculations well beyond and beneath the proper
province of their work, defining such speculative essays as "counterfactual." That is an entirely false term. History does not consist
of "facts" but of statements of them. "What if?" is a better term,
allowing speculations of something not really "counter" but
plausibly divergent from the actual result of past events. The
proper words are *plausible* and, especially, *actual,* words more
telling than *definite,* since every actuality — implicitly, or around
its edges — also suggests potentiality.† This or that event hap-

---

* *Inevitable, unavoidable, predestined* do not exactly have the same mean-
ings: but that is a linguistic and epistemological question.
† This corresponds to the most important recognition of quantum physics: that the actual existence of an atomic particle is inseparable from its po-

pened; and it could have happened otherwise. But that "otherwise" must include plausibility; it must have been possible and plausible. The great Dutch historian Johan Huizinga once wrote: "The historian . . . must always maintain towards his subject an indeterminist point of view. He must constantly put himself at a point in the past at which the human factors still seem to permit different outcomes. If he writes of Salamis, then it must be as if the Persians might still win." Two decades ago I chose this passage to be the epigraph and motto of my book *The Duel,* dealing with the history of the eighty days between 10 May and 31 July 1940, since at that very time Hitler had come close to, he could have won his war. What if Hitler had subdued England in June 1940? This "what if?" is not a "counterfactual" question. It is admissible, because the success of Churchill's and Britain's defiance of Hitler was not inevitable.

Another great historian, Owen Chadwick, once wrote that there is a mystery in every historical event. That, I think, accords with the great (Portuguese) proverb "God writes straight with crooked lines." So it was with many events of the Second World War — for example, that the Red Army was a most powerful element in a war that Hitler lost and the Western democracies won.

Let me now ask a painful question that I have often asked myself: was the Holocaust inevitable? No. Let me put this reasonably: what if there had been no Holocaust? — more precisely: no planned and completed murder of six million Jews and other victims during the Second World War? What if Hitler and his minions had chosen to sequestrate and corral and deport Jews

---

tentiality — an important conjunction of physics and history. Readers who wish to pursue this further may look at the "Physics and History" chapter of my book *Historical Consciousness.*

and other victims of Germany from much of Europe into miserable concentration camps, but not proceed to kill most of them—whereby most Jews and other victims in Europe and in the western Soviet Union would have survived the war?* Well, there is one certain answer I think I can give to this—not at all implausible—potentiality. It is that, if so, after the war and surely now, sixty or more years later, the reputation of Hitler and of National Socialism would be much better than it is. So these hecatombs of the dead, these "crooked lines" have had at least one "straight" result. (Even those who deny, or argue to diminish the extent, of the Holocaust do not quite say that, yes, there was a war, and the Jews got what they deserved.)

A last remark. There are still millions of people in Europe, including Germany (and presumably on other continents, too), who admire Hitler. (We have seen that certain "right-wing"—an imprecise designation—parties in some countries may gather as much as 15 to 20 percent of the vote.) It is remarkable that their leaders and members are silent about Hitler. They do not invoke or even mention his name—presumably because of caution, or to avoid punitive or legal consequences? But their silence about Hitler does not mean his repudiation. And: will there be a rehabilitaiton of Hitler in the future? I—we—cannot tell.

---

* Hitler did think that Jews and his other dangerous opponents must be expelled; but by 1941 there was no way to gather and send them to some faraway places at the end of the world; they had to be liquidated: for what would they do if, God forbid, his Germany lost the war?

The Place of the Second World War — At the End of an Age

The widespread appellation Second World War suggests the second of a series, the second chapter or perhaps even the continuation of the First World War. There are reasons for this formulation, but our perspective must be wider. Nineteen forty-five, the end of the Second World War, marked many things. It was the end of a period of great wars; it was the end of the European Age; it was the end of colonial empires; and perhaps the end of the entire Modern Age.

If by "world war" we mean a war between great states that is fought across seas on more than one continent, then the wars between France and Britain throughout most of the eighteenth century, and perhaps even some of the wars among England, Spain, Holland, and France during the seventeenth, were world wars. The war that began in 1914 was at first the "European

War" — so it was named in Britain in the first (1915) official British publication of documents. Soon it was obvious that this war was to be fought not only on the high seas but beyond Europe, also on other continents. Yet it was not just geography but the general impression of its tremendous size and nature that made the epithet of World War, *Weltkrieg*, become swiftly widespread (mostly by Americans and Germans), in 1915. When we come to the war begun in 1939, again there is some reason to call it a European War before 1941 — that is, before the full involvement of Russia and Japan and the United States — yet it was called the Second World War from the beginning. Let us now eschew the not entirely unreasonable argument according to which this war began not in 1939 but in 1931 or 1937 with the Japanese invasion of Manchuria or China — but that was not a world war until the active involvement of other world powers in 1941.

All the world wars of the past centuries involved the ambitions of one great power to dominate Europe or at least the western half of it, with Atlantic consequences: this was Spain and then France and then, after a century unscarred by world wars, Germany trying twice. All of them European powers; all of them with colonies overseas. After 1945 no longer. What the Germans called 1945 — *Jahr Null*, Zero Year — involved more than their utter defeat at the end of the Second World War. It was also the ending of the British and of other European empires, and in Asia of the Japanese one; the end of most colonies; the end of the European (as distinct from the Mediterranean) Age.* At the end of the cold war Russia, too, had to abandon most of its imperial

---

* *Europe* and *European* (as distinct from *Christendom*) became gradually accepted terms after 1450–1500. Geographically, too, the Mediterranean ceased to be the principal theater of history, as it had been for three or four thousand years before 1500.

holdings. The United States remained — the ultimate victor of the last world wars, and especially of the Second.

But the scope, the purpose of this book is not an overview or a sketch of global history. It is to assess the historical place, and meaning, of the Second World War. Was it a continuation — a continuation, even more than a consequence — of the First? And, later, was its nature — were the conditions of its warfare — wholly different from all of the world wars that had preceded it?

◆ ◆ ◆

The responsibilities of the principal perpetrators of the First World War were divided; for the Second World War they were not. At the end of July 1914 Austria, Serbia, Russia, Germany, France, Britain; monarchs, prime ministers, foreign ministers, generals, admirals, chiefs of staffs; press lords, politicians, journalists; public opinion and popular sentiment — all of such, in nearly every country, were responsible for what was happening and what was about to happen. On 1 September 1939 one man took the decision, Adolf Hitler. The responsibilities of other governments and of other peoples — when and if they existed at all — were, at worst, those of omission, not of commission. They were different from Hitler's. In 1914 the responsibilities of different states and governments were differences in degree.

Still — in 1914 Germany (its rulers, its government, its people) was more instrumental in choosing war than were other states. Because of this both 1914–1918 and 1939–1945 were — as we now know, the last — attempts by Germany to dominate much of the continent. That would have been the result if Germany had won the First World War — and even if that war had come to a standstill through a compromise peace between Germany and her Western opponents. (Proof of this is the short-lived "peace" treaty of Brest-Litovsk in 1918, forced by Germany on her weak and revolution-ridden opponent Russia.) Nearly a century after the First World War there are historians, not German ones (Niall Ferguson), who suggest that not going to war against Germany in 1914 would have led to a more or less united continental Europe of a kind that some Europeans are trying to tack together now. Such "What if?" speculations about history have their limits. They must remain within the framework of potentialities that are reasonable only because of historical evidence. Yes, Germany's war aims were not limitless (nor were they in the Second World War: Hitler wanted the Third Reich to rule most of Europe and European Russia, and perhaps some of the eastern Atlantic, but not other continents) — still, had Germany won the First World War, the world would be very different even now.

Consider something that lies both beyond and beneath politics and warfare. This involves the — in retrospect, astonishing — vitality of the German people. Defeated in 1918, and suffering the deepest shocks and crises for years afterward, they recovered so that the — senseless as well as severe — restrictions imposed on them by the Versailles peace treaty were losing their effects rapidly. It is telling to look at the record of the, otherwise inconclusive, negotiations of German and French and other diplomatic delegations about rearmament and other provisions of the Versailles Treaty in 1931 and 1932, at a time when hardly anyone expected Hitler coming eventually to power. The record suggests that the German delegates sensed that their negotiating power was already equivalent, if not superior, to that of the other negotiators. In sum, this sense — as yet unspoken but more and more felt — was that Germany was rising again; that the shackles imposed upon it in 1918 were rusting and cracking; that in a few years, perhaps toward the end of the 1930s, Germany was about to become again the greatest continental power within Europe, with or without a war. The language and the behavior of German diplomatists during these negotiations in 1931 and 1932 is telling — at a time when the worldwide Depression smote Germany deeper than any other nation, when Germany struggled under a torn political system, with weak governments, masses of unemployed workers, street fighting, and so on. In these last years before Hitler the rise of neither him nor German power can be explained by economics, by financial or industrial statistics. Not even the numbers of German demography can explain that strange and sullen phenomenon of the people of Germany Rising Again. Something more was happening there, both above and beneath the visible surface of the mainstream of events.

◆ ◆ ◆

During the nineteenth century Germans bore more children than the French. In the eighteenth century France had the largest population in Europe; one hundred years later there were almost twice as many Germans as French. Of course much of this was owing to the fact that while in the past France had been a united state and Germany had not, after 1871 there was a united Germany — and there were millions more people outside the German state who identified themselves as Germans. There was even more than that. Germany became the most industrial, the most productive state in Europe. In 1900 German products surpassed in quantity (and sometimes even quality) those of Britain, only recently "the workshop of the world." That, too, was the result of something more important than raw materials and methods of production. The Germans were now a much-schooled people; their formal education was perhaps the best in the world. When in 1870–1871 the French were beaten by the Germans, Ernest Renan wrote that the German victory at Sedan was the victory of

German schoolmasters — an unusual admission by a French philosopher, but there it was. Many states throughout the world adopted German models of schooling and teaching. Beyond the universities of Germany new generations of intellectuals appeared who were impressed by German philosophy, science, music, thought. This was so in countries such as Spain, Greece, Italy, Russia; of Marxists as well as of conservatives.

What is more telling for our purposes is that this continued after Germany's defeat in 1918. By the 1920s no longer Paris but Berlin was the cultural capital city of Europe, pulsating with all kinds of new experiments. The last great intellectual achievement of the Modern Age, a revolutionary recognition of new realities in physics, took place in Germany in the 1920s.

An analysis of the German educational system is insufficient to explain this. The Romantic reaction against the cold rationalism of the French eighteenth century, against the so-called Enlightenment, was, more than often, German. German thinking at its best (and also at its worst), including art and philosophy, whether Wagner or Nietzsche, represented a reaction against the bourgeois materialism of the nineteenth century. Neoidealism was the great German contribution to the intellectual history of Europe, ranging from philosophy to physics. Entire generations were sympathetically attuned to this, even when, politically speaking, they were not Germanophiles. Other millions, whether within Germany or without, sometimes only half-educated, admired the dynamic efficiency of Germans as cultural prototypes, representing the wave of their present, if not of their future.

All of this proved to be a great advantage for Hitler's Germany before (and at least for a while during) the Second World War. But before we get to that we ought to consider that long before the Russian Revolution in 1917 and the other minuscule revolutions thereafter, the Age of Revolutions in Europe was over. It was largely over in 1848–1849, after the last wave of democratic revolutions that had begun on both sides of the Atlantic and in Western Europe after the 1770s. What followed was a series of wars, wars between nations rather than struggles between classes. Bismarck foresaw that much better than many others, including Marx. Yet there was a difference between Bismarck's thinking and that of many Germans, including Hitler, two generations later. Bismarck thought in terms of possible wars between states. What followed after him, already in the First World War, were wars involving states, yes, but more than that of entire nations. Hitler understood this. He was not able to apply this new condition entirely to his foreign policy; but he was able to apply it almost entirely to his own people. That was a result of his recognition that ideas are more important than matter; indeed, that ideas determine matter.* This idealist determinism carried him far. It was the source of many of his stunning achievements and successes; but then it was source, too, of his disaster and of Germany's ultimate defeat.

That he rose to power in 1930–1933 because of the economic depression is a widely accepted thesis but one that is superficial. One noteworthy element in the history of those roiling and seething crisis years in Germany is that, alone among the political parties at that time, Hitler's National Socialists had not much of an economic or financial program. Still, our subject is the Second World War, not German history; it is not Hitler's arrival to power but his exercise of it. And his exercise of power, his political and military leadership, were inseparable from his idealistic

---

* His very "racism" ought to be examined more closely. He was an extreme nationalist rather than a racist. (There are many evidences of this. See especially page 102.)

determinism. He believed that he would — more, that he must — come to power in Germany because he and his National Socialists and National Socialism were stronger than any of their opponents, because they not only represented but incarnated an idea and ideals that were more powerful than those of the others. Thus he won Germany; thus he won — almost — his European war. Some time in April 1940 he talked with Goebbels. They agreed that this war was but a repetition, on a larger scale, of what had taken place in Germany during their ascent to power. In those years a National Socialist street fighter was worth two Communists or three Social Democrats. Now a German soldier was worth two or three of his French or British opponents. Hitler's Germans were bound to win — yes, because of their discipline, equipment, training: but, first of all, because they incarnated ideas that were better, more dynamic, more attuned to the present than those of other peoples. Let us not dismiss this as foolishness, the hubris of a fanatical ideologue. General Alfred Jodl, who was no fool, and who saw earlier than others that the war was no longer winnable, said in 1943: "We [Germany] must win, for otherwise world history will have lost its meaning." Field Marshal Model, one of the best German generals, said in March 1945, close to the end: "In our struggle for the ideals of National Socialism it is a mathematical certainty that we will win, as long as our belief and will remain unbroken."*

We must not fool ourselves. Hitler's National Socialism was more than one of many elements in the history of the Second World War. It was the origin of the Second World War; it led to astonishing German achievements (and to unbelievable German

---

* He shot himself a month later when an American army surrounded his group in the Ruhr.

crimes) during the Second World War. It brought Hitler very close to winning during the first two years of the war.

◆ ◆ ◆

Hitler's National Socialism was an Austro-German phenomenon; but the alliance of nationalism and socialism was more universal. It both preceded and succeeded the Second World War. Our subject is not a study or essay of the political movements of the twentieth century; but I am compelled to treat that alliance (at times an engagement, at other times a veritable marriage) briefly. Both nationalism and socialism came out of the democratization of the world that Tocqueville foresaw, examples of which reach back to centuries even before the Modern Age. Nationalism began to affect masses of people during the nineteenth century, at first commingling with variations of old-fashioned patriotism and eventually replacing it. Socialism, the recognition by people and parties and, in the end, governments that the state must provide some kind of support to the mass of its working populations, was adopted, more or less willingly, by ever more governments, in one way or another, before, during, and after the First World War, whether or not they adopted the name Socialist. What Hitler recognized was that socialism can and must be national and not international,* that the struggles of classes meant less than the conflicts of nations, that the sentiments and ideas of people, anchored within their nationality, were stronger and deeper than propositions of their material conditions. In sum, he proposed a marriage of nationalism and socialism — but with the emphasis on the former.

The very word *Nazi* proves this. Hitler's followers were national, not international, socialists; hence their abbreviated name

---

* And that "capitalism," too, must be unreservedly national in its purposes.

in the 1920s (originally a designation with a somewhat sarcastic tinge): Nazi-Sozi. Very soon the *Sozi* faded out; the *Nazi* remained. Rightly so: Hitler's "Nazi" nationalism — and its appeal to many people both within and beyond the Germanies — was more important than his and their socialism. It was populist and popular.* It was thus that nationalists and populists in many countries and states rallied to Hitler's side both before and during the Second World War — at times against their own governments' struggles to maintain their independence from Germany. A prime example of this was in Austria, where the so-called Nationalists were pro-German, against the principle of the independence of their state, and for uniting its people with Germany.

Here we come to one fundamental difference between the First and the Second World Wars. The First World War was still principally, and often entirely, a war between states, not between classes, and not between adherents of different political ideas or sentiments. In 1914–1918 there were, here and there, people bitterly critical of their governments: but hardly any who sympathized with the enemies of their country, who wished for the defeat of their state. (The only exceptions to that were some of the non-German and non-Austrian and non-Hungarian people and soldiers of the Austro-Hungarian multinational empire; and that, too, became significant only near the end of the war). But in 1939–1945 there were millions of internal, not only external, enemies of their governments, Communists in different states

---

* Sixty, seventy years after Hitler and his Third Reich, many people are still confused about this — whence the imprecise and obtuse employment of the word *Fascist* to cover all, past and present, phenomena of "the extreme Right." (Not to speak of the stupid designation of Hitler and Hitlerism as "reactionary.") Mussolini came before Hitler and later became his ally: but one fundamental difference between the ideology of the two — we must add: popular — dictatorships was that Mussolini tried to enforce in Italy the primacy of the state, Hitler in Germany the primacy of the *Volk,* the people.

across the world whose sympathies (and, on occasion, allegiances) were to the Soviet Union. There were other millions whose sympathies (and, on occasion, allegiances) were for Hitler's Germany and Imperial Japan.* These were not insignificant minorities. One example: tens of thousands of Frenchmen and Frenchwomen, and perhaps millions of non-Germans in Central and Eastern Europe, wished for the victory of Germany as late as 1945. There were of course other millions in those same countries, majorities in some, minorities in others (and some indeed within Germany itself), who wished for the defeat of their government and for the victory of its enemies, of Britain or America or Russia, if must be.

We have seen that the Second World War, 1939–1945 — and, in a way, the history of the world at least during the quarter-century 1920–1945 — was marked by a great triangular contest between parliamentary democracy, Communism, and radical nationalism — represented and incarnated by, respectively, the English-speaking nations (and some others), the Soviet Union, and Germany (and some others) and Japan; and it took the strange alliance, the unusual† combination of the first two to defeat the third in a great war lasting many years. This triangular struggle of powers was also repeated across the globe, within many states. In China, for example, there were three forces (and during the war, three actual governments); one in Chungking,

---

*They were not "Fascists," because both before and especially during the Second World War there were no non-Italians who wished for the triumph of Mussolini's Italy.

†Well, perhaps not so unusual. Nineteen fourteen: the Western democracies and Tsarist Russia against Imperial Germany. In the sixteenth and seventeenth centuries, at least at times: Protestant England and France against Catholic Spain. But nationalism, though existing, was not the *main* issue then.

another in Nanking, a third in Yenan province, the first a pro-Allied one led by Chiang Kai-shek, the second a pro-Japanese one, led by Wang Ching-wei, the third a Communist one, led by Mao Tse-tung.

There was yet another element of divided sentiments and allegiances. Beyond and beneath ideological politics there were Germanophile people and Anglophile people (or, conversely, Germanophobes and Anglophobes) whose sympathies or antipathies related to Germany or Britain as cultural prototypes. (One example: many of the Pétainist armistice partisans in France in 1940 were French Anglophobes rather than French Fascists.) In many other countries, such distant ones as, say, Rumania or Argentina, men and women of the upper middle classes tended to be, by and large, Anglophiles; those of the lower middle classes Germanophiles. Russophiles, even among Slavic peoples, were few. The results of these, by no means superficial, divisions were virtual and, in some cases, actual civil wars in many countries near the end (and, on occasion, even beyond the end) of the Second World War.

Since 1945 it has become a commonplace to say that the German generals were among the best, if not the best, in the Second World War. Perhaps, but German soldiers, too, were among the best, if not the best, through the war. In the summer of 1942 Winston Churchill himself mused, sadly, that British soldiers in this war were not what they had been during the First. Germans were as good, indeed often better. But: was this so because they were National Socialists? In some cases: think of the Waffen-SS (and of its more than one hundred thousand non-German members): their at times admirable courage, at other times contemptible brutality—the latter a result of their contempt for their opponents and victims. In more cases, no: for it was their nationalist discipline, not National Socialism, that kept most of the German people and most of their soldiers together till the end — when they feared that the end of this war meant the end of the Germany they knew, the only Germany they could imagine. That was the reason (if *reason* is the right word, which I fear it is not) why thousands of German civilians, many of them not committed Nazis, chose to commit suicide at the end of the war. (Among Communists few, perhaps even none, chose to kill themselves when the Soviet Union and other Communist governments collapsed in 1989 and after.)

One reason why nationalisms and their history is more interesting than socialism is that the development and the essential features of the former vary from country to country, and from one culture to another. Thus the sources and the outcomes of Japanese or Chinese nationalism are not the same as European or American ones. Such differences may be subjects of anthropological and sociographical studies dependent on a profound acquaintance with peoples of the Far East, for which this is no place and for which this author is unequipped. However, we must take a rapid glance at Japan, whose soldiers, sailors, airmen fought with a fanatical dedication in the Second World War. Even more than among Germans, during the war there were instances when masses of Japanese chose suicide rather than surrender to their enemy (and this could have happened in the event of an American, or Russian, invasion of their homeland). But: for the Japanese their nationalism was inseparable from their worship of their Emperor, which saved them in the end. And what then happened in Japan was not altogether different from what happened to other allies of Germany, Italy, or Rumania or Bulgaria or Hungary,* which surrendered to the massive weight of Germany's enemies before they were invaded or conquered entirely. This happened because of monarchs and their advisers who were not National Socialists and who decided to act thus to protect their countries and peoples from the protracted ravages of extreme nationalism.

◆ ◆ ◆

We have seen that, at least in the beginning, the British called the First World War a European War, even though it was fought in Africa and in the Pacific from its beginning.† So began the Second World War, too. In 1939 Germany had no colonies in other continents — also, unlike in 1914, Japan had not entered the war against a European Power. (True: Canada, Australia, and New Zealand declared war on Germany in 1939.) Hitler wanted to rule most of Europe — and perhaps later, the European part of Russia. He was not much interested in colonies; he would not wage war for German conquests in the Western Hemisphere; he did not (at least not until 1941) wish to destroy what was still then the British Empire. What he hoped was for a Britain (and a weak France) that would accept such a German domination of Europe, or of most of it. That, largely because of the accumulated reputation of the limitless nature of his ambitions, did not happen. However reluctantly, the British and the French declared war on him in September 1939, because of his invasion of Poland. Till the last minute Hitler hoped that that the British would relent. Also, in September 1939 there was no patriotic or

* In Hungary it was a regent, not a king, who attempted to detach his country from Germany and surrender — but his attempt failed miserably.
† Some British people sometimes called the Second World War the second German War (imprecisely, though not altogether wrongly).

nationalist enthusiasm for war, not even in Germany. The memories of the First World War were still too close and too strong.*
But then came Hitler's astounding victories, the rapid wars won in Poland, Denmark, Norway, and then in Holland, Luxembourg, Belgium, and France.

But here we come to a difference between the two world wars. Had the Germans captured Paris, to which they came close in September 1914 and in April 1918, the war would have continued, France and Britain (and in 1918 the United States) would have fought on. A German military victory over France would not have been a *total* victory. But in May and June 1940 Hitler came very near to winning a total victory in this war, his war. One man, Churchill, stood in his way. Hitler and Goebbels knew that.† Churchill knew that too. To approach Hitler would mean Britain reduced to a servile state, at best a junior partner of Hitler's Germany.‡

"Of course, whatever happens at Dunkirk we will fight on." Brave words, and more than words, a brave resolution. Note that this happened before the large-scale withdrawal of the British Army from Dunkirk. But: had the Germans captured the nearly three hundred thousand British troops at Dunkirk; had Hitler then offered to return them to England in exchange for the British people's stopping the war; had the Germans actually invaded

---

*There was one similarity between 1914 and 1939. In 1914 most of the German military leaders thought that if war was to come, better then than later. In 1939 Hitler thought that time was working against him (a calculation also because of his thoughts about his health). He was wrong.
†Goebbels in his diary a year later, 18 June 1941, about Churchill: "Were it not for him, this war would have ended long ago."
‡He did not say this publicly; those words he uttered in confidential meetings with the War Cabinet and the outer cabinet; see my *The Duel*, p. 99, and *Five Days in London*, pp. 4–5, 183.

England during that summer, he would have won his war. But that moment passed.

There was yet another moment when he came close to winning his, still mostly European, war. That was in September and in October 1941. Stalin was compelled to write Churchill: "The Soviet Union was in mortal danger," on the verge of collapse. In 1918 the Germans forced Russia out of the war, and yet they could not win it in the West. Nineteen forty-one was different. Had Hitler forced Stalin to give up, he would have been unbeatable; and Churchill's and Roosevelt's resolution to keep fighting Germany could have been untenable. But in early December his armies had to halt in the winter before Moscow at the same moment when half a world away in the sunlit Pacific the Japanese attack propelled the United States into the war. Such a turning point did not occur during the First World War.

That was the end of the European war and the full beginning of a world war that Hitler could no longer win. But here we arrive at a very important point, which is that Hitler himself knew that. This is contrary to the accepted view, according to which he was blinded by his own fanaticism, hoping and thinking till the end that his Germany must win. There are many evidences that he knew and understood what was happening—as early as mid-November 1941, that is, before the last difficult attempt of his Army Group Center to make a lunge toward Moscow. On 19 November he dropped a remark to General Halder, then chief of staff: "The recognition, by both opposing coalitions, that they cannot annihilate each other leads to a negotiated peace." Four days later he said, also noted in General Halder's War Diary: "We must face the possibility that neither of the principal opponents [Germany and Britain] succeeds in annihilating, or decisively defeating, the other."

He knew that. But his temperament was mercurial. He still

thought he could win. Or, more precisely, that his lightning wars were over. Now his entire strategy changed. Germany must be prepared for a longer war. From now on he and his armies would fight on with unbreakable toughness that would bring them victories in one theater or another, on one side of the war or on another — and then the unnatural coalition of British and Americans and Russians, of capitalists and Communists, would break apart. Such was the strategy of his great idol Frederick the Great, such was to be his. He ordered his armies in Russia to stand fast, to brave the terrors of the Russian midwinter. He ordered, too, the transformation of the German economy to a more or less total wartime basis. (The change of the German policy from the expulsion to the extermination of Jews in Europe was also finalized at that time.)

We shall see that the Anglo-American-Russian coalition indeed began to break up at the end of the war; but too late for Hitler. Until then these disparate Allies had agreed on one thing: that Germany must be conquered and occupied in its entirety. Yet that was to take almost four years. If in November 1941 Hitler thought that he could no longer win his European war, he also thought that he was not condemned to lose it. On the night of the news of Pearl Harbor his great adversary Churchill thought that Britain, finally and well nigh inevitably, was now destined to win. Yet a few months later, in the summer of 1942, he and Stalin and even Roosevelt could still have lost. For six months after Pearl Harbor the British and the Americans in the Far East and in the Pacific were retreating and reeling from defeat to defeat. In the central Pacific in June the aerial battle of Midway was an American victory, but yet nowhere else. In North Africa General, now Field Marshal, Rommel defeated the British from time to time and was about to enter Alexandria and Cairo, where and beyond which Egyptian and other Arab populations were ready to cheer his Germans as deliverers. What could have been a giant German pincer closing in on the Near East moved ahead in southern Russia, advancing to the Volga and into the Caucasus. There was no Second Front in Europe, relieving the Russians who were struggling against more than two million advancing Germans and German allies, while the British were in combat against fewer than two hundred thousand Germans (and Italians) in the western desert near Egypt.

It may be that the greatest danger was not that of the battle-fronts — it was that Stalin might attempt a separate peace or armistice with Hitler. In August 1942 Churchill flew across three continents for the purpose of reaching Stalin in Moscow. There it was not only his revelation of the news of a coming Anglo-American invasion of French North Africa that succeeded to impress and — somewhat — to assuage Stalin. It was also the impression that Churchill's combative personality made on him. (It is difficult to imagine any other British personality who would have been able to impress him thus.) A fortnight later the British army in western Egypt, now led and commanded by General Montgomery, halted Rommel's Germans. Two months later the military turns in the fortunes of the war arrived, coincidentally, at four points of the globe. In the battle of El Alamein the British forced the Germans to begin to retreat across North Africa. The Americans (and some British) landed in French North Africa. The Russians encircled a German army around Stalingrad. The Japanese were halted in New Guinea and Guadalcanal. November 1942 was the military turning point of the Second World War. But Churchill warned his people: it was not the beginning of the end, it was but the end of the beginning. It took another two and a half years to conquer Germany, and even more to force the surrender of Japan.

◆ ◆ ◆

This is a history not of the Second World War but of its place in the history of the world in the twentieth century and perhaps in the entire Modern Age. Europeans discovered Japan in the very beginning of that age, in the sixteenth century; but a century later the Japanese rulers chose a sullen isolation. More than two hundred years later its rulers decided to enter the Modern Age around the same time (1868: the so-called Meiji revolution) that the German Reich became the greatest power on the European continent (1870), and so it remained in two world wars. Japan rose to the status of a Great Power in 1894, remaining so for fifty years. It defeated first China and then Russia, and became a World Power about the same time as the United States, if by World Power we mean a state whose possessions extend across the seas to other continents.

For the first half of the twentieth century one factor in the history of the world was the dissolution of China. Japan took more advantages of that than any other power, including Russia. When the great war in Europe broke out in 1914, Japan entered that First World War at its very beginning (among other things, as Britain's ally), taking hold of the few German imperial possessions on the China coast, and then extending its sphere of influence to China, and building a modern navy whose size in the Pacific was second only to that of the United States.* The increase of Japanese naval power in the Pacific and, even more, Japanese ambitions in China disturbed the United States. When the latter decided to establish diplomatic relations with the Soviet Union in 1933, an unspoken accord between Stalin and Roosevelt was their common interest in watching the further expansion of Japan. Yet that expansion went on in stages. From a

---

*In 1917 Japanese destroyers appeared in the Mediterranean along with British and French and Italian warships.

Chinese perspective the Second World War began in September 1931, when the Japanese occupied Manchuria—a principal portion of China—and erected a satellite state there. Next year they resumed their consquest of the China coast. When the Second World War broke out in Europe in 1939, Japan had already controlled most of the coast of China, along thousands of miles (and all of Korea that Japan had conquered thirty years before); Japanese rule extended all the way from Russia's Far Eastern frontiers to those of French Indo-China (with the solitary exception of Hong Kong, a last British dot on the enormous flank of the Far East). The Japanese could not of course occupy all of China, even as their power seeped inland from the coast here and there. Their ambition was to make China a weak and fissiparous state, a satellite of the Japanese Empire. But in 1940, unlike in 1914, they had to face the possibility of war with the United States. They would not attack the United States and its possessions in the western Pacific, but they would advance against the remnants of the French, the Dutch, and possibly the British colonial empires in the Far East.

Yet—who were "they"? There was an unspoken, and often hardly apparent, division among the rulers of Japan, not unsimilar to the division within the ruling circles of other states in regard to Hitler's Germany. The emperor and some of his advisers were conservative, which meant that they were unwilling to promote a war with Britain and the United States. Other political figures, especially the Japanese military, were fierce with their admiration of the new dynamic Germany. For a while (again, as in many governments and states of Europe) anti-Communism was a cement that bound the ruling powers of Japan together; but they had to reconsider their aims directed at the Soviet Union, whose Far Eastern borders in Mongolia they had probed by military means in 1938 and 1939, when the

Russians pushed them back; and then, lo and behold, anti-Communist Germany signed a pact with Stalin's Russia. But when in September 1940 Hitler offered Japan an alliance, Tokyo accepted that instantly. That year the Japanese began to push into French Indo-China; in April 1941 they made a nonaggression pact with Russia. Ten weeks later Hitler's Germany invaded the Soviet Union. Thereafter the Japanese proceeded to a fateful decision, probably the worst taken by any Great Power in the Second World War. They examined two prospects and three possibilities of action: attack northwestward and invade the Soviet Union, or move southward, against the remnant French and Dutch and British possessions in southeast Asia, facing an eventual war with them and even with the United States; but meanwhile keep the, increasingly difficult, negotiations with the United States going for the next six months at least. They chose the move to the south, not east. The result, five months later, was the great Pacific war, starting with Pearl Harbor and other astounding Japanese victories, but ending with the destruction of the Japanese Empire and the occupation of all of Japan by the United States.

Here we must eschew the complicated history of Japanese-American negotiations that preceded Pearl Harbor during which neither side was altogether innocent. Nor must we sum up the dramatic history of the Second World War in the Pacific and in the Far East, ending with the American atomic bombs cast on two Japanese cities and the (often neglected) effect of the Russian declaration of war against Japan, after which the conservative emperor took matters into his hands and told his people to accept their defeat and end the war. We must, instead, consider the consequences of 1945, looming large in the history of the world in which we live. It was because of China, principally because of China, that America chose the prospect of war with Japan in

1941; China was the stumbling block in those negotiations in which Washington required that the Japanese give up just about all of their previous conquests in China. Before and throughout the war the United States and Britain supported a pro-Western Chinese government, while Japan installed a pro-Japanese one; Russia supported the Chinese Communists, though not very effectively and with some reluctance. Yet in the Chinese civil war, developing almost immediately after the surrender of Japan, a civil war not unsimilar to what was happening in Greece or Yugoslavia at that time, but a civil war in which neither the Russians nor the Americans wished to be much involved, the Chinese Communists won by 1949. What happened after that — the Korean War; Russia's withdrawal from its bases in China; the prospect of a Russo-Chinese war; and, eventually, American amity with China — is beyond our scope, except perhaps to note that while in 1945 the two great victors in the Far East were America and Russia, a few years later Russia was a loser and the United States still a relative winner — of sorts.

Much more important for our purposes is what the Second World War brought about first in Asia and then across Africa: the end of colonialism, that of the British, French, and other European empires. Much of this did not only come about as a consequence of the war but developed already during it. In 1939 the prestige and the power of people of the white race still existed throughout the world, but here and there their weaknesses were becoming evident. After all, the Japanese had defeated a Russian army and annihilated a Russian fleet already one generation before 1939; and — a small but not insignificant evidence — in 1939 and 1940, when the British government had finally decided to stand against Germany, it felt compelled to make concessions to Japan in China. In 1941 the British were still able to crush an anti-British (and pro-German) revolt in Iraq; and even in the bleak month of August 1941 a few British and Russian troops, in conjunction, could occupy Persia (Iran) in a few days, getting rid of a potentially anti-British and pro-German shah. But the dejected and shameful British surrender of Singapore to a small Japanese army in February 1942 was the death knell of the British Empire in the Far East, a loss of British prestige that would not be extinguished entirely but would never return close to its previous heights. All through East Asia the native, nationalist, and anti-colonial leaders and their followers received Japanese support; with few exceptions, their appeal survived the defeat of Japan. In 1942 Churchill said that he had not become prime minister to preside over the liquidation of the British Empire; three years later he was no longer the prime minister: but no matter who would govern Britain after the war, the convictions for empire had weakened among the British people well before the war, and had no support from either the American government or people before or during or after the war. That the American people did not and do not think of the United States as an imperial power is another matter: but that does not belong to the history of the Second World War.

◆ ◆ ◆

The Second World War began between Germany on the one hand, Poland and Britain and France on the other. Its ultimate victors were the United States and Russia. Churchill was the one who did not lose it in 1940; Roosevelt and Stalin won it in 1945. The United States and Russia did not come into the war until 1941; but already in 1939 the shadow of their presence grew across Europe. Twenty years before that both the United States and Soviet Russia, for different reasons, had withdrawn from Europe. In 1939 Stalin found that his Russia was being courted, indeed, invited into Europe by France, Britain, and then Germany — with the prospect of regaining almost everything that the tsar's (and Lenin's) Russia had lost after the First World War. In 1939 Roosevelt had already decided that the United States must support Britain and France, indeed any state that opposed Hitler — including the prospect that the United States would one day enter the war. This inspired Churchill and the British people throughout most of 1940 and 1941. They preferred to be dependent on America, not on Germany. If the price of the American alliance with Britain was a piecemeal transfer of British possessions to the United States, so be it. The very day Hitler invaded Russia, 22 June 1941, Churchill declared that Britain was now Russia's ally. Roosevelt thought the same thing, though he was more cautious to declare it openly because of the still widespread isolationist and anti-Communist sentiments within the American people; but he ordered to extend the same kind of material and armament support to the Soviet Union as was being given to Britain. Then, as the war went on, American enthusiasm for the Russians' fighting ability grew, especially among the American military; and American material and armament shipments to Russia became a veritable flood, especially by 1944, when the Russians no longer needed that much; but then such is the momentum of machinery, perhaps especially in the democratic age.

As the war went on Roosevelt thought that his relationship with Stalin was even more important than his already established relationship with Churchill. At times he acted accordingly, on occasion at Churchill's expense. One reason for this was obvious: Russia must not drop out of the war — indeed, one day Russia must join America in warring against Japan. The other element in Roosevelt's mind was less reasonable. He saw the Soviet Union, with its Communism, as a rough pioneer society and state, representing at least something of the future — and therefore he saw America moving somewhere midway between what was old

(Britain) and what was new. (Churchill, to the contrary, saw Russia not ahead but well behind the peoples of the English-speaking world, and Stalin as a kind of peasant tsar.) Roosevelt's view, even if wrong, was shared by much of American public opinion, at least during the war. Stalin, too, favored Roosevelt, and respected the material power of the United States. At Yalta in 1945 he agreed that the Soviet Union would enter the United Nations (that was Roosevelt's favorite idea, a new international-ism beyond Wilson's previous illusions); also that Russia would enter the war against Japan three months after the surrender of the Germans. (He kept his word to a T.) At Yalta, too, they agreed on a Declaration of Liberated Europe — which, in prac-tice, amounted to a tacit acceptance of Russia's domination of much of Eastern Europe. Churchill understood what that meant; so did Stalin; Roosevelt not quite. Out of this came the cold war and the "iron curtain" (Churchill's phrase),* a year or so after Yalta, which in 1945 had been cheered to high heaven by many Americans.

Before that, and still before the end of the war in Germany, there occurred a symbolic event. On 25 April 1945 advancing American and Russian troops met near Torgau, along the Elbe River, cheering and drinking and celebrating into the night. Among this mass of soldiers there were some young Americans who had come from the American Far West, the shores of the Pacific; and, presumably, some Russian infantrymen who had come from the Russian Far East, from lands along the Pacific. So they encountered each other in Torgau, in the middle of Europe and in the middle of Germany. This, indeed, was not the end of

---

* He had not originated that phrase, which first appeared here and there around 1921 (when the new Soviet Russia closed off its frontiers from the rest of Europe). It was also enunciated by Goebbels in early 1945.

Europe but the end of the European Age of history. Most of Europe was now divided by Americans and Russians. Their reciprocal misunderstanding of what that meant became soon apparent; but the cold war was only a consequence of the Second World War (which does not belong in this particular chapter). Here is suffices to state that Roosevelt's successor President Truman's thinking about Stalin and Russians was not like Roosevelt's. Among other important matters Truman did not allow the Russians to partake in the occupation of Japan even after they had contributed to its defeat and surrender.

A last remark: while the Americanization of much of Europe was largely spontaneous, a Russification of Eastern Europe did not happen; and even the Communization of much of Eastern Europe proved transitory in the long run. Less than fifty years after the Second World War, Communism and Russia's presence in Eastern Europe were gone. How long the American presence and Americanization will prevail no one can tell.

◆ ◆ ◆

Before 1939 people, including some military experts, believed that air power (more precisely: aerial bombing) transformed the very nature of future wars. Air power, sea power, land power: that would be the order of their relative importance. This was not what happened — not within Europe and Russia, which were, after all, *the* decisive theaters of the Second World War, and not against Germany either. Against Japan, yes: American air and naval power, in conjunction, won that war (even though on land the Japanese fought and may have fought not only until but beyond the bitter end). In the Atlantic and east of it the Allies had to subdue the Germans' packs of submarines; also, it was their naval supremacy that enabled them to cross the Channel largely undisturbed in 1944, something that Hitler could not do four years earlier. Yet after D-Day the essential matter was the presence and the movements of large Anglo-American armies. The strategic bombing of Germany, involving the destruction of entire German cities, did much harm to German industrial production but could not decide the war. Aerial firepower could be decisive tactically, not strategically: in other words, when airplanes functioned as flying artillery over and behind battlefields. Both sides recognized this on the eastern fronts, where there was little or no strategic bombing. One week after D-Day the Germans could employ another strategic aerial weapon, their rockets. They caused much harm but changed nothing in the outcome of the war. By that time the Allies (including of course the Russians) knew that their mass armies would have to overrun and occupy Germany in its entirety. We must admit that it was Hitler who recognized early the new supremacy of land power — whence his Blitzkrieg strategies, and his admiration for the internal-combustion engine that made it possible to move troops faster on land than by sea (which the British had been able to do for at least two centuries, including in their wars against Napoleon).

War on land involved something else too. During the Second World War the rules distinguishing combatants from noncombatants, soldiers from civilians, disappeared. More civilians than soldiers were killed during the Second World War. Soldiers and airmen and armed policemen killed civilians but then, on occasion, civilians killed soldiers too. It is possible to produce a, necessarily quite imprecise, total number of the mass of armed people who lost their lives from September 1939 to August 1945; it is not possible to give more than a vague total of the civilian (more precisely: nonmilitary) casualties. Their sum total was certainly larger than that of the military personnel.

Here was one of the great and deep differences between the

First and the Second World Wars. During the First World War entire nations fought each other; it was — already — a war of peoples; civil populations suffered during the war but, except for certain instances in Eastern Europe, they were not systematically attacked and killed. There was the long-range firing at Paris by enormous German cannon in 1918; these was frequent German mistreatment of Belgian people; there was the shelling of Scarborough and Hartlepool by German warships in 1914; but these occasions were exceptional and sporadic. Elsewhere noncombatants lost their lives only when they lived or found themselves in places where battles between armies raged. Even there few women and children lost their lives, even though their lives were endangered or they were maimed by a lack of food sometimes amounting to partial starvation (many instances of which occurred after the war). There were not many civilians who attacked foreign soldiers occupying their land; there were also few soldiers who were engaged in killing unarmed noncombatants. (One large exception was the Turkish massacre of Armenians in 1915.)

The Second World War was different. The (mostly unwritten, though sometimes codified) rules of the "civilized" or "limited" warfare of the preceding two centuries disappeared. Some of the — relatively civilized and at times even chivalric — manners of professional armies remained, but these were exceptions. After many centuries, barbarism returned — indeed, here and there it became widespread and general. The largely indiscriminate bombing of enemy cities increased gradually, until it reached enormous proportions. Beyond the bombing of particular industrial targets (something that was, for a long time, inaccurate and therefore not very effective), the targets of bombing began to encompass large portions of entire cities, with the aim of destroying the routine lives and work of their populations together with the vague expectations of breaking their morale through chaos. The Royal Air Force dropped a few bombs on German cities in the summer of 1940; during the aerial Battle of Britain, Hitler and Göring switched their strategy to the bombing of London and other British cities in September. The British (and later the Americans) began their massive bombing of German cities in 1942, culminating later in the large-scale destruction of Hamburg and Berlin and Dresden; the Germans retaliated by firing unstoppable rockets on London and Antwerp in 1944 and 1945. Hundreds of thousands of people were killed and burned, but the expectations of aerial warfare were not satisfied: strategic bombing was not enough to destroy either the enemy's production or its people's will to go on. (In some cases people proved that they were the opposite of raw meat: the more they were pounded the tougher they became.)

There were exceptions to that. In July 1943 the first bombing raid on Rome contributed to the decision of the king and of others to get rid of Mussolini. In the German-Russian war strategic bombing was rare. In the war against Japan massive bombing was not decisive — until the two atomic bombs in August 1945 (which, however, were not the *only* reasons why the emperor decided to give up the war). In March 1945 American bombers destroyed much of Tokyo (the number of dead, perhaps 145,000, was as large as the combined total of Hiroshima and Nagasaki), yet the Japanese fought on. Japanese suicide bombers (the so-called Kamikaze) flew themselves into American warships that year. There were no such volunteers anywhere else, and certainly none during the First World War.

But now the involvement of volunteer fighters as well as that of noncombatants became widespread on land. Here and there — especially in Eastern Europe, but also on certain islands in the

Pacific — thousands of civilians were killed by the invading armies. During the Russians' march into Germany and Central Europe perhaps hundreds of thousands of women were raped by Russian soldiers; hundreds of thousands of men were taken away to slave labor or prison camps. The active reaction against the Germans' occupation in France (and in other Western European nations) became represented, indeed, incarnated in the phenomenon of "resistance" (which, come to think of it, is a conservative word). Its effectiveness varied from country to country and from time to time; but it meant something new in the history of modern warfare. Civilians were now bearing arms, attacking soldiers. Telling cases were in Yugoslavia and Greece, where the Germans eliminated the state armies in record time, but a few months later it appeared that national resistance against the occupiers had not been extinguished; soon the Germans had to face a guerrilla war. That was a new phenomenon of the Second World War; yet also something that amounted to a revival of the phenomena of nationalist or tribal banditry that had existed in the Balkans a century or so before. The men and boys of the Home Army in Poland and its rising in August 1944 incarnated something inspiring. In the end the Germans chose to recognize some of them as combatants (also for political reasons).

Other instances involved the suppression or deportation of entire national populations. The Germans attempted to eradicate the presence of Poles from some of the western provinces of Poland; Stalin ordered the deportation of Volga Germans in 1941, and of Crimean Tartars and Chechens in the Caucasus in 1944 and 1945. To this category of national sequestrations or deportations belongs the, of course much less brutal and more humane, decision of the American government and judiciary to collect and concentrate the Japanese-American population of the

West Coast (including American-born Japanese) and transport them to camps inland, from which they were allowed to return at the end of the war.

None of these instances of sequestration or suppression compares to the destiny allotted to the Jews of Europe and of European Russia by the Germans. I now arrive at the mass murder (a term preferable to the abstract word *genocide*) of Jews during the Second World War. The enormity of what this meant did not appear to many people until 1945, when the American and British armies overran some of the German concentration camps. An important difference between the German mass murder of Jews and their killing of other civilians was that while the latter victims often were found to have been engaged in fighting, their Jewish victims were largely innocent. But many Germans (and many other Eastern Europeans) saw the Jews as their enemies. By and large, the German people were less Judaeophobic than, say, Ukrainians or Rumanians; only convinced Nazis among the Germans believed that Jews were by their nature evil. What most Germans thought (if they chose to think about this at all) was that Jews were adversaries of Germany in this war.

On a level of sentiments that was by and large so. But this is not the place to attempt an analysis of German convictions and sentiments. What we must look at are the successive phases, the development of the German industry of murder. The original Hitlerite policy was the expulsion (more exactly: the enforced emigration) of Jews from Germany: because of this more than two-thirds of the Jews of Germany (and of Austria) had left by 1940 and thus saved their lives (and in some cases even some of their possessions). But soon large portions of Eastern Europe fell under German occupation; and that was where most Jews of the world still lived. While elsewhere German policy still allowed for an ever smaller number of Jews to leave Europe, in Poland

Jews were corralled into ghettoes; and in early 1942 the first gas halls and crematories were set up. Some time around September 1941 the main German policy changed from expulsion to extermination. In January 1942 a high-level conference agreed to gather and transport Jews from almost all of Europe to such camps in Poland. The result was the mass murder of more than five millions Jews during the last four years of the war.

The motives and the purposes of Hitler and Himmler during the development of this awful, often unspeakable and unthinkable, process were more complicated than what, at first sight, may seem to have been a simple-minded fanaticism (I shall return to this in Chapter 4). In any event the consequences of this ghastly portion of the Second World War were large and enduring. By 1950, for the first time in history, more Jewish people lived in the Western Hemisphere than in Europe, where now no state had a Jewish population much larger than 1 percent. The second and allied consequence was the end of the British mandate and rule in Palestine and the establishment of the state of Israel in 1948, surrounded by hostile populations and states. A third consequence was the unacceptability (and unspeakability) of anti-Semitism in the Western world (though not in Russia, especially not under Stalin) — whereby it may be said that after the horrors inflicted on Europe's and Russia's Jews during the Second World War, there rose a kind of golden age for Jews in many places, perhaps especially in the United States — one of Hitler's unintended consequences indeed.

◆ ◆ ◆

There were of course other consequences of the Second World War throughout the world. Their consideration may illuminate certain matters beyond a narrative, suggesting their relative importance. And while there is a difference between significant and important events, there is one too between immediate and long-range consequences,whether large or small.

One large consequence: the peak of American power. In 1945 the size of the United States Navy alone was greater than that of all other navies of the world combined. The United States had the monopoly of the atomic bomb. The American dollar was the single dominant and stable money in the world. After 1945 the Americanization of much of the world became ever wider, together with the increasing American military presence on at least three continents. Even before the end of the Second World War two American inventions changed the nature of international relations. One was the atomic bomb, which made great wars between Great Powers largely unthinkable. The other was the United Nations, a pet idea of Franklin Roosevelt. Roosevelt wished to go better than his predecessor Wilson's League of Nations and establish the United Nations as the main instrument of a new world order and world peace. Like the League of Nations, the United Nations soon fell short of fulfilling such American expectations. Still, it was symptomatic as well as symbolic that in 1947 its headquarters was erected on the brute flank of New York City, to which Stalin did not object at all, even as the cold war had by then begun.

There were other, more enduring, consequences of the Second World War in Europe. Perhaps the most important of these occurred in Eastern Europe, in many countries of which considerable German and Jewish minorities had been living, in some cases for more than eight hundred years. The brutal reduction of the number of Jews was followed by the migration and expulsion of German minorities westward, after which the German and Jewish presence in Eastern Europe largely ceased to exist. In the center of Europe, Germany, though having lost large territories to Poland (and in one instance to Russia: Königsberg and its hinterland), was — contrary to some wartime expectations — divided temporarily: the Russian occupation of eastern Germany where a Communist satellite state existed for about forty years but not more. It is noteworthy to consider that the political map of Europe, meaning the existence and the extents of states, changed relatively little after the Second World War. After the First World War four great empires (the Austrian, the Ottoman, the German, the Russian) either entirely fell apart or became greatly reduced in size, while almost a dozen new or enlarged states in Central and Eastern Europe came into existence. After the Second World War, many frontiers remained unchanged. It was not until after the end of the cold war that two of these states, Czechoslovakia and Yugoslavia, set up in 1918, broke apart.

After the First World War the Near East changed even more drastically than Eastern Europe. The chaotic dissolution of the Turkish Ottoman Empire went on for five years, involving a larger portion of the globe than for any of the other three former empires. Yet most of the results of this grandiose redrawing of the map of the Near East (some of it drafted by Winston Churchill, British colonial secretary in 1921) have remained to this day: artificial and other entities such as Iraq, Jordan, "Saudi Arabia," Syria, Lebanon, Palestine, and a Jewish homeland are extant states even now. Consequent to the Second World War the British and French presence in some of them ceased to be; yet by and large, these — often artificial — states have gone on existing.

◆ ◆ ◆

Our knowledge of history is revisionist by its nature. Yet the application of the term *revisionism* to history is relatively new. It became current after the First World War and the peace treaties following it. It meant the political intent to review the unjust features of some of those treaties. *Revision,* in the *Oxford English Dictionary,* is "the action of revising or looking over again; esp. critical or careful examination or perusal with a view of correcting or improving." The related entries there do not mention historians; they mention "revisionists" who in the 1860s and in 1888 wished to revise certain texts of the Bible. In Germany "revisionists" were those Social Democrats who around 1875 chose to revise the categorical Marxist doctrine of the inevitability of a proletarian revolution. But more telling for our purposes was historical revisionism, directed at the injustices of the record, at revising the widely accepted tenets about the origins of the First World War, about Germany's primary and principal responsibility for it (among other matters, stated in the Treaty of Versailles). The Germans had good reasons to combat that. As early as 1919 the new republican German government began to publish documents in order to prove that the guilt for the outbreak of the war in 1914 was not Germany's alone. More extensive and scholarly documentation was published in a series of volumes a few years later. Germans felt so strongly about this that in 1923 a German amateur historian, Alfred von Wegerer, began to issue a scholarly journal, *Die Kriegsschuldfrage* (The war guilt question). Soon other writers and historians, especially in the United States, took up the cause of revisionism about the First World War. More than ninety years after 1914 matters about the origins of the First World War are still occasionally discussed by historians, though *revisionism* and *revisionists* are no longer applied to them.

Sixty years and two generations after the Second World War things are simpler. No Hitler, no Second World War—more precisely, no Second World War begun in 1939. This is hardly arguable. Yet argued some of it is, sometimes subtly, sometimes less subtly, by serious, mostly German, historians* — who, while not defending Hitler, state that Polish intransigence and British hostility strongly contributed, if not led, to the outbreak of the war in September 1939. Their purpose accords with the purposes of those German historians whose writings led to the Historians' Quarrel in 1986–1987, to qualify or to reduce the German responsibility for the crimes of the Second World War — an understandable and, in some instances, justifiable impulse. Still, the arguments of some of these "conservative" or "nationalist" historians are questionable. They include three, occasionally connected, theses. One is that the crimes of the Third Reich were not unique, if we consider those committed by the Soviet Union (perhaps tenable, except when a German historian such as Klaus Hildebrand claims that there was no such thing as National Socialism, only Hitlerism). The other, connected, argument, especially pursued by Ernst Nolte, is that not only had Russian Bolshevism preceded German National Socialism but the latter was really a reaction to the former. The third, argued by the late Andreas Hillgruber but also by others, is that after 1939 Britain was intent to destroy Germany: an argument at least relating to the more widespread and popular German Two-War Theory (about which see Chapter 5), according to which Germany's war against the Western powers, especially against Britain and the United States, was perhaps avoidable and regrettable, but by fighting Soviet Russia Germany acted as a bulwark and defender of European and Western civilization, a service that Germany's Anglo-American enemies, blinded by their hatred as they then were, regrettably failed to recognize. In the 1990s there came another, fourth, revisionist wave — in this case involving the

* Examples: Dietrich Aigner, Oswald Hauser, Andreas Hillgruber, Ernst Nolte, Rainer Zittelmann.

origins not of the war in 1939 but of the German-Russian war in 1941. Depending on newly appearing Soviet documents whose provenance and authenticity are often questionable, Germany and Austrian and Russian writers have argued that Hitler's attack on the Soviet Union in June 1941 was a preventive move, since Stalin had been making ready to attack Germany at that time or shortly thereafter — an interpretation that found a few scattered supporters even in the United States as also elsewhere, despite its lack of serious substance.

Still — the origins and the record of the Second World War are debated less than were those of the First. Hitler's responsibility and the often criminal actions of his regime are — at least publicly — seldom mitigated or questioned.* Lately we have seen even such odd phenomena as the political leaders of Germany presenting themselves at commemorations of D-Day and V-E Day, side by side with Germany's former enemies, in Normandy and in Moscow.†

More than sixty years after 1945 neo-Nazi parties and symbols are still forbidden in much of Europe, while Communist ones are not; the printing and the publication and the sale of *Mein Kampf* and of other such books is illegal, while Marx's and Lenin's and

---

* In the Far East, Japanese nationalism and its interpretation of much of the Second World War in the Far East *is* revisionist; but it exists only within Japan, where a popular consensus either does not exist or is not ascertainable.

† Until now even those who admire Hitler seldom appear in public as his defenders. Their intention, rather, is to blacken and incriminate his chief adversaries, usually Churchill. Their method is often a careful and knowledgeable falsification of documents that seep into later publications after they have been inserted into archives (rather than filched from them). The purpose of their, often clever, fabricators is — or should be — obvious: to contribute materials to an eventual revision of the history of the Second World War.

Stalin's writings are not; the display and the wearing of Nazi and other similar flags are not permitted while Communist symbols are — and why? Because of the danger of their potential popular appeal?* Will this kind of selective indignation — or, rather, anxiety — disappear after a while? We cannot tell. There has not been a great extent of revisionism about the Second World War, after all. Nor has there been any serious revival of Hitler's reputation in the past sixty and more years. Will this always remain so? Communism has now lost much of its reputation, but what still goes on by the (imprecise) names of Capitalism or Globalization is bound to result in considerable opposition and thus enter a crisis. Might not a third alternative arise and appeal to people, one not identical with what was National Socialism, but with an inclination to rethink, to give some credit to the latter? This book is the work of a historian, not of a prophet.† But history is not only potentially revisionable; it is also unpredictable. And most people, including historians, will always be prone to adjust their ideas to circumstances — for so much easier that is than to adjust circumstances to one's ideas . . .

* It is worth noting that the press, almost everywhere, is especially sensitive to evidence of extreme right-wing appearances, more so than to such manifestation of extremism on the "Left."
† I have sometimes thought that if Western civilization melts away, if it collapses during a rising flood of barbarism, Hitler's reputation may — I write "may," not "will" — rise in the minds of some people, as a kind of Diocletian, a last architect of an imperial order; and he might be revered by at least some of the New Barbarians.

THREE

The Division of Europe

The division of Europe was one of the main results of the Second World War. It was not only one but *the* main cause and condition of the following cold war. But before attempting to describe the development of that condition, we ought to ask the question: was there a "Europe" in 1939? The answer must be ambivalent: yes and no.

Yes, there was a Europe in 1939 as it had been for a long time. But geographically not more than a peninsula of Eurasia; indeed, the geographical definition of Europe was made as late as 1833 by a German geographer drawing its boundaries. He divided "European" Russia from Russia's Asian empire, along the crest of the Ural Mountains (which corresponded to no political or municipal or regional borderline within that empire); he included in "Europe" the large isthmus of the Caucasus, the entirety of which Russia had only recently conquered. Of course, the idea of "Europe" was much older than that—though not *very* old: the word *Europaeus* appeared only toward the end of the Renaissance. And the stunning recognition that Europe was but a peninsula of Asia arose in the minds of a few Europeans only around 1900, as they saw the rise of Japan and the United States to the status of world powers — that is, states whose colonies and other possessions now extended to other continents, a condition that had been the privilege of certain European states before that.

But: was there really a "Europe" in 1939? Europe is of one piece only when people look at it from the outside. The national differences were profound. From Albanians and Andorrans to Bulgarians and Belgians: there were more European states (and of course nations) than there are letters of the alphabet. Few of their populations thought of themselves as Europeans; even fewer considered themselves as principally Europeans — significantly fewer in 1939 than ten years before. The main reason for this was the impact of National Socialism, which, in different ways, revived the convictions and sentiments of various nationalisms.

If there were fewer "Europeans" in 1939 than in 1929, it may even be argued that there was more of a "Europe" two hundred years before — that is, before the rise and the presence of populist nationalisms. The notion and the sense of "Europe" in the eighteenth century was aristocratic and intellectual; its nearly universal language was French; it was current mostly among men and women of the upper classes and neither universal nor uniform. During the nineteenth century the greatest statesmen within Europe, Metternich and Bismarck, thought and occasionally said that *Europe* was too vague a term, not really a political reality — but they also believed that Europe mattered so much more than the rest of the world. There was also the ambivalence of two of the greatest powers on the edges of Europe: Britain that was of, but not in, Europe; Russia that was in, but perhaps not quite of, Europe.

The First World War changed much of that. We saw that because of its magnitude it soon bore the epithet of a World War. Still, it was fought mostly within Europe and decided on battlefields in Europe. A condition arose during the First World War that would recur during the Second, a condition that led to an actual division of Europe. In 1914–1917, as in 1814–1815, and again in 1941–1945, the Western Allies needed to keep Russia in the war. To assure that they felt compelled to allow Russia large territorial gains in the east of Europe. In 1916 the French (and also British) confidential concessions to Russia included even Constantinople—as well as other not clearly defined potential Russian gains largely consequent to the eventual breakup of the Austro-Hungarian Empire and to the eventual defeat of the German one.* In 1917 the Russian Revolutions, especially the second, Bolshevik, one in November, relieved the Western Allies from these promises and commitments. No one saw this advantage at the time, fearful as they were, not unreasonably, both of Communism and of Russia dropping out of the war against Germany. Yet in 1918 the Western Allies, with the United States, were able to defeat Germany even without Russia. Two years later, for wholly different reasons, both Russia and the United States retreated from Europe—the new Russia because it was forced to do so, the United States because it wanted to. There

---

*Before 1917 the aims of Tsarist Russian foreign policy were not unlike Stalin's during the Second World War: Russia ruling much of Eastern Europe, British and French domination in Western Europe, and a weak and divided Germany in between.

was now a semblance of a "new" Europe, without Russia and without the United States.

But it was only a semblance. Much in European life and in European finances was influenced by America. And, as we have seen — again for different reasons — in 1939 the shadows of the United States and of Russia reappeared over the European theater. There was, however, another difference. The horrible experience of the First World War, for which the old order, or disorder, of Europe's leaders were all in varying degrees responsible, led, for a while, widespread opinion that this must never happen again, and that the instrument for a peaceful and reconstructed Europe must be some kind of unity. A pan-European movement (founded by Count Coudenhove-Kalergi, an Austrian nobleman with Greek and Japanese forebears) gathered support in many European countries, and well-meaning noddings of heads by many reputable statesmen. "Pan-Europe" proposed some kind of a union between the states and nations of Europe, though without Britain and Russia. If in the eighteenth century some kind of a notion of "Europe" was current mostly among certain aristocracies, in the 1920s it was current mostly among the cultivated middle classes and some intellectuals. That it was not altogether superficial may be glimpsed by a meaning that the adjective *European* had acquired, even before 1914, in the languages of Central and Eastern European nations. A "European" was a person with a certain level of cosmopolitan education, nonnationalist (though not necessarily nonpatriotic), representing a certain level of "European" civilization and culture.

That was not superficial; but it was ephemeral. By 1933 pan-Europeanism disappeared, melting away like a small pat of butter in the sizzling skillets of nationalism. During and after the Second World War it reappeared, in other ways and forms. But the theme of this chapter is not a history of the "European" idea. It is the division of Europe during and immediately after the Second World War.

◆ ◆ ◆

In 1938 Hitler's Germany became the greatest power in Europe. None of the other powers, including Britain, were ready or even willing to challenge that, surely not at the risk of another great war. The unanswered, and perhaps unanswerable, question was: were there any limits to Germany's expansion eastward?* The British and French governments chose not to confront that question until March 1939, when Hitler, unnecessarily, broke his word given at Munich and decided to occupy what remained of Czecho-Slovakia. There now occurred a kind of revolution in British (and French) public opinion: Hitler must be told not to go further. That was not only a mutation of sentiments. There was a realistic calculation inherent in it. It went back to memories of 1914, when one of the reasons for the German decision to plunge into war was the uncertainty of what Britain would do. Now, in 1939, there must be no uncertainty. The result was a British guarantee to (and later, alliance with) Poland (and also Rumania and Greece), the first such commitment ever of a British government to an Eastern European state. Hitler hoped that the British (and, in their wake, the French), irresolute and weary of war, would accept his domination of Central and Eastern Europe — but now, because of Poland, this would not happen.

Suddenly the issue was more than Poland. It involved Russia. For the first time after twenty years this dark, sullen, and isolated Communist state found itself approached, if not courted, by

---

* There *was* an unspoken distinction. If Germany would invade any country west of Germany, the Western powers would challenge that by war, when needed. German expansion in Eastern Europe was another matter.

the main powers of Europe. Poland, for good reasons, wanted nothing like an alliance with her sinister barbarian neighbor. Yet without Russia, could the British and the French prevent Germany from overrunning Poland? Stalin realized that Hitler could offer him much more than the Western democracies would. The result was his refusal of any kind of alliance with the West. Instead, he reached out and made a pact with Hitler. Stalin, more and more conscious that he was a Russian statesman rather than an international revolutionary, could now recover for Russia many of the lands that his predecessor Lenin had lost twenty years before. The outcome was a division of Eastern Europe between him and Hitler, including the fourth partition of Poland.* In August and September 1939, in a secret protocol, a geographic line drawn up by Moscow, allotting to the Soviet Union the eastern half of Poland, the unfortunate three Baltic states, Finland, and a slice of Rumania that had belonged to Russia before 1918.

That division of Eastern Europe largely prevailed until Hitler chose to invade Russia in June 1941. Before that Stalin hoped to extend it to southeastern Europe, to the Balkans. After having conquered Western Europe in the spring and summer of 1940, Germany began to incorporate Hungary and Rumania and then Bulgaria and eventually Yugoslavia into its own sphere of interest—while in the north Finland was slipping out of the Russian sphere. Stalin asked Hitler to allot at least Bulgaria to him. (He also thought of making a second sphere-of-interest division of the Balkans with Mussolini's Italy, but Hitler forbade it.) Before 22 June 1941, the day of Germany's invasion of Russia, almost all of the continent of Europe had been conquered or was allied to Germany in one way or another; the only

_____
* The first three: 1772, 1793, 1795.

exceptions were the three neutral states of Portugal, Switzerland, and Sweden.

Meanwhile, there was another division that Hitler had in mind, not in the east but in the west. This was nothing less than a division of the globe — or, rather, of the Eastern Hemisphere. If Britain would accept Germany's domination of Europe, Hitler would leave the British Empire largely intact. In May 1940 this made some sense. Churchill, to his everlasting credit, refused to consider that. He not only thought that accepting a Europe ruled by a single state would deny centuries of British history and tradition; he also knew that this would reduce Britain to a junior partner of Hitler's Germany at best, or a "slave state" at worst. What Pitt said in 1805 Churchill could have said in 1940 and after: "England saved herself by her exertions; and Europe by her example." Almost alone among British political leaders Churchill was a "European" (worth stating in our times, when so many British Conservatives are anti-European).* As early as July 1940 he said: "We are fighting *by* ourselves alone, but not *for* ourselves alone." London was "this strong City of Refuge which enshrines the title-deeds of human progress and is of deep consequence to Christian civilisation." Yes, London was more than the capital city of Britain and of the Empire then. It was a bastion city of a free Europe. Its streets were enlivened by the various uniforms of Polish, Norwegian, Belgian, Dutch, Free French soldiers. The queen of Holland, the king of Norway, the grand duchess of

---

* Yes: he could "not maintain the Empire. . . . Those who call this failure ought, perhaps, to propose alternative policies that might have prevented the relative decline of British authority in a much enlarged world. The British Empire was the product of an unrepeatable combination of historical factors, and far from it being the case that Winston mortgaged Britain's future to wage World War II, in fact he spent a windfall inheritance to assure a future for values the civilized world regards as eternal." This profound assessment by the British historian Richard Holmes.

Luxembourg, the president of Poland had come to live in London and survive the war. The British Broadcasting Corporation carried the voices and sounds of a free Europe; its broadcasts beamed to Europe began with the first bar of the Fifth Symphony of Beethoven.

And yet: could Britain survive without American help? And: could Britain liberate Europe—all of Europe—alone? In 1940 the second of these questions did not call for an answer. However: it involved Russia. Stalin and his Russians were now Hitler's partners. However: they had their own interests. Churchill (and the British) knew that. For instance, their guarantee to and alliance with Poland, which then led to the British declaration of war against Germany, was a guarantee against Germany, not against Russia. When in September 1939 Stalin invaded Poland from the east, no matter how dismaying, there was no British countermeasure to that. Churchill thought that sooner or later Hitler would invade Russia, rendering the latter, no matter how, an ally of Britain. Even before that event in June 1941, we may detect a consistency in Churchill and the British view about the eastern part of Europe, indeed about Europe at large. Churchill saw that the alternative to Germany ruling all of Europe was a Russian rule in much of Eastern Europe; and of course half of Europe (especially its western half) was better than none.

On 1 August 1941 an editorial in the London *Times* read: "Leadership in Eastern Europe can fall only to Germany or Russia. Neither Great Britain nor the United States can exercise, or will aspire to exercise, any predominant role in these regions." The *Times* was not necessarily a spokesman for the British government, but that government was beginning to defer to Russia. What the geographical extent or limits of that Russian "leadership" would be—these were not, and could not, be Churchill's main preoccupations at that time. But he had to face these questions, in one way or another, as the war went on. There was the overall condition that both he and Roosevelt understood. They were dependent on Stalin, on the Russian armies throughout the war — even at and after D-Day in 1944, when two-thirds, if not more, of the German armies were struggling against the Russians in the east.

However — in 1941 there were at least five months when Stalin's dependence on Churchill and Roosevelt may astonish us in retrospect. He had become enough of a statesman to judge the overall prospect of the war at least as well as they did, with a realism that could be harsh on Russia, but so be it. On 31 July 1941 he said to Harry Hopkins, whom Roosevelt had sent to see him: "The might of Germany [is] so great that, even though Russia might defend itself, it would be very difficult for Britain and Russia combined to crush the German military machine." The United States must enter war against Germany. Also: he "would welcome American troops on any part of the Russian front under the complete command of the American Army." Six weeks later he sent a message to Churchill: the Soviet Union was on the verge of collapse. Could not Britain send twenty-five divisions to Russia, under British command, if need be?* Obviously

---

* One example of Stalin's wish to make any kind of concession at that time: on 3 August 1941 he asked Roosevelt to put pressure on Finland to detach itself from Germany. "In this event the Soviet Government would be willing to make to Finland certain territorial concessions as to facilitate her transition to a peaceful policy and the Soviet Government would be willing to conclude with Finland a new Peace Treaty." This was a time when the geographical and political limits of a future Russian expansion in Eastern Europe could have been ascertained, agreed upon, fixed. But: can we blame Churchill and Roosevelt for not paying much attention to that at the time — when the German armies were streaming toward Moscow, when the battle of the Atlantic was entering a critical phase, when an American war with Japan was impending? I fear that we cannot.

he was ready to make any concession to his new Anglo-American allies, in order to survive. But then he survived, and the balance — who depended more on whom — immediately changed.

◆ ◆ ◆

One problem was Poland. The British, and especially Churchill, felt a moral obligation to Poland, not only because of their 1939 guarantee but because of their active alliance. Almost 150,000 Polish soldiers, sailors, and airmen were fighting on the side of Britain in different places. There was, too, the exiled but legal government of Poland in London, with a considerable authority, much more than a cabal of exiled politicians. Soon after June 1941 Stalin agreed to reestablish diplomatic relations with it. But the Poles had many reasons to worry about Russia. In March 1942 Churchill talked calmly and confidentially to their excellent leader Władysław Sikorski. He said "that his own assessment of Russia did not differ much" from that of Sikorski. But he could not afford to confront or quarrel with Russia. "He underlined the reasons which made it necessary to conclude an agreement with Russia. She was the only country that had fought against the Germans with success. She had destroyed millions of German soldiers and at present the aim of war seemed not so much victory, as the death or survival of our allied nations. Should Russia come to an agreement with the Reich, all would be lost. It must not happen. If Russia was victorious she would decide on her frontiers without consulting Great Britain; should she lose the war, the agreement would lose all importance."*

An agreement about which Churchill and Sikorski were talking was one proposed by Stalin in December 1941, only a few days after the military tide had turned before Moscow. Windows

---

* *Documents of Polish-Soviet Relations, 1939–1945* (London, 1961), pp. 267–268.

in the Kremlin were still occasionally rattling from the sound waves of cannon not far away. Anthony Eden arrived in Moscow with drafts of an Anglo-Russian declaration. Stalin said that he wanted an agreement, not a declaration. "A declaration I regard as algebra, but an agreement as practical arithmetic." He produced a detailed Russian draft agreement about the Soviet Union's frontiers after the war, replete with secret protocols — in essence a British acceptance of the western frontiers of the Soviet Union in June 1941, most of it along the German-Russian partition line arrived at two years before. Knowing the Americans' objection to secret treaties, the British told Stalin that they could not make commitments in such terms, without stating explicitly that they would oppose them. When the division of Europe came up later in the war, Stalin found that he could profit even more from American algebra than from British arithmetic. That American algebra was the Declaration for Liberated Europe made at Yalta, amounting — contrary to American ideas — to the division of Europe.

But, before getting there, we ought to consider that the main matter was not where the postwar frontiers of the Soviet Union would be. It was, rather, what Russian rule in Eastern Europe would mean. As far as Poland went, Churchill was much aware of that. He wanted to agree to the Russian incorporation of prewar eastern Poland* in exchange for a Russian commitment to a pro-Russian, but democratic, non-Communist regime in the rest of Poland, a Poland also to be compensated with territories taken from prewar eastern Germany. He failed, because of Russian (and also because of Polish) intransigence. In April 1943 the

---

* Which contained millions of non-Polish populations beyond the so-called Curzon Line (which had been temporarily proposed by Britain and France in 1920 and that also largely ran along the German-Russian partition line of 1939).

Russians, on a pretext, broke their relations with the legal Polish government in London. Thereafter they began to collect and establish a postwar Polish regime composed of Communists and pro-Communists wholly dependent on Moscow. For two more years Churchill, increasingly alone (meaning: not supported by Roosevelt), struggled to save something of a Polish democracy but in vain.

Meanwhile — throughout 1941 and 1942 and 1943 — Stalin demanded a Second Front. He saw that Russia was carrying the brunt of the war. The relative inactivity of the Western Allies on land, together with their reluctance to launch an early invasion of Western Europe, filled him with anger and suspicion. That was his main concern at least until the end of 1943. It is at least interesting to speculate: what if he had had his wish? Had Anglo-American armies successfully invaded Western Europe in 1942 or 1943, overrunning Germany, and meeting the Russians some-where well in the middle of Eastern Europe, then — would Stalin have objected? Hardly, or not at all. He was a nationalist tyrant, rather than an international revolutionary. He thought that Russia deserved to rule much of Eastern Europe and perhaps also a part of Germany after the war. "Rule," for him, meant uncondi-tional subservience to Moscow, for the assurance of which he thought he could mostly count on certain Communists, many of whom he otherwise regarded as hardly more than toadies, hardly above (and at times even beneath) contempt. As a statesman, he believed in the necessity, indeed, in the desirability, of a partition of Europe. So did Churchill — though along different lines. Roo-sevelt and the Americans did not.

◆ ◆ ◆

The differences between the American and the British ideas, plans, prospects about Europe during the war are, in retrospect, significant: but decisive they were mostly not, because they were seldom at the top of the agenda of their leaders. There was the overall American insistence that no political commitments or treaties should be made until after the end of the war — an insistence that was abstract and legalistic and impractical and at times disregarded by the Americans themselves. This attitude was at the same time inseparable from the then overwhelmingly pro-Russian tendency of American public opinion, as well as that of President Roosevelt, who thought that much, if not indeed everything, must be subordinated to the maintenance of the alliance, to the need of the best possible relations between the United States and the Soviet Union. A result was that both the American government and the American people began to realize the division of Europe and the dangers of Russia's expansion not too early but too late.

A partition of Europe (though never admitted thus) was already a consequence of important decisions made at Teheran in December 1943, the first summit conference of Stalin, Roosevelt, and Churchill. The first two got what they wanted most: Stalin a commitment that the great Anglo-American invasion of Western Europe would finally come in May–June 1944; Roosevelt a commitment that Russia would eventually enter the war against Japan. Churchill was already concerned with what he saw as the main issue of the war in Europe: whose armies would meet and stand where at the end of the war? It was more and more evident at Teheran that Roosevelt was not supporting Churchill, especially not when it came to Churchill's inclination to what could be seen as his marginal strategy: to invade Europe from the south, perhaps even in the Balkans, and extend the very slow Anglo-American progress through Italy. It is noteworthy to observe that in Teheran, Stalin did not seem to be much bothered by this — even though he recognized that Churchill was anxious and perhaps even reluctant facing the prospect of a great invasion and then a monstrous struggle with German armies in France. Stalin was also pleasantly aware of Roosevelt's disassociation from Churchill on more than one occasion. So far as the future of Europe was concerned, Churchill achieved one thing: a unanimous declaration for a future independent Austria — a small matter then, but eventually quite important during the development of the cold war.

The division of Europe and the partition of Germany, though concurrent and largely interdependent, were not the same thing. For example, Churchill at Teheran brought up his idea of dividing Germany into three or four of its once historical components; he also proposed a kind of Danubian confederation consisting of Bavaria and Austria and perhaps even Hungary. Stalin at least did not object much, while Roosevelt's thoughts about the future of Germany were different — but, in any event, the partition of Germany was not discussed further. Still, some arrangements had to be prepared for the eventual occupation of Germany at the end of the war, a matter that at Teheran and even later was seen as temporary and marginal; yet there are so many things in life that seem temporary and then become permanent. Such was the agreement to draw up zones for the temporary occupation of Germany along lines that took on the look of permanence. "Temporary," yes: but the division of Germany (and of Europe) lasted more than forty years.

Even before Teheran it was agreed that a European Advisory Commission, set up in London, would draw up the occupation zones in Germany (later that was extended to Austria). This commission, to the work of which relatively little interest was paid, consisted of ambassadors and experts beneath the rank of their foreign or prime ministers. Their discussions were protracted but not hampered by severe disagreements. The main lines of the occupation zones were drawn up in the late spring of 1944. They followed precedents from earlier world wars, especially those of the occupation of France and Paris after Napoleon's fall, when France was temporarily divided into Prussian, Russian, Austrian, and British occupation zones, with the eighteen arrondissements of Paris also divided by these four, and accordingly a rotation of the military governors of Paris every month. (Something similar was drawn up by the Allies in 1915, too, before the Dardanelles and Gallipoli, for a planned occupation of Constantinople.) Unlike France in 1815, and unlike at the end of the First World War, now Germany would be occupied in its entirety, divided into Russian and British and American zones of occupation. The Russian zone would encompass about 40 percent of the territory of prewar Germany, with Berlin in its middle — which, like Paris in 1815, would also be divided into three occupation zones, symbolizing Allied cooperation and unity.* These arrangements were not unreasonable. Consider that they were reached before the Anglo-American invasion of France, when it was at least conceivable that at the end of the war the Anglo-American and Russian armies would meet up somewhere along the Rhine. A similar plan about the zoning of Austria was not made until January 1945, according to which each of the four occupation powers was allotted two of the eight provinces of that state.

It is interesting that during the protracted negotiations of the European Advisory Commission a main problem was caused not by the Russians but by the Americans. President Roosevelt, anx-

---

*A year later this had three amendments. France was given an occupation zone (taken from the original American zone). In East Prussia the city of Königsberg and its hinterland were given to Russia. The sovereignty of (of course pro-Soviet) Poland was extended to the Oder-Neisse Line, about which see page 79.

ious about American popular sentiments, wanted to keep the American occupation zone the smallest of the three, one in northwest Germany around the ports of Bremen and Hamburg, to facilitate the shipping home of masses of American soldiers at the end of the war. The British objected to this, for more than one reason.* Oddly enough, the Russians supported the British. In the end the Americans accepted a large zone allotted to them in southern, southwestern, and central Germany.

This again suggests a difference between Roosevelt's and Churchill's thinking. Roosevelt separated, or tried to separate, military from political considerations. Churchill did not—especially as the war in Europe seemed to be nearing its end. Churchill believed that where the armies were at that time might well nigh decide where a partition of Europe would occur. This would be so especially in the east of Europe. So, even before D-Day, he thought of doing something. He knew that Russian occupation of a country would lead to its eventual Communization, in that order of sequence. Two possible exceptions to that were Greece and Yugoslavia, where native Communist or Communist-led guerrilla forces were strong. (He was especially concerned about Greece, a traditional ally of Britain, because a Communist-led mutiny had already occurred among Greek warships stationed in Alexandria in April 1944.) Meanwhile, Russian armies were approaching the Balkans. Churchill offered Moscow a British agreement to recognize the primacy of Russian interests in Rumania and Bulgaria, in exchange for Moscow's recognition of a principal British interest in Greece. Again the main problem was Washington, not Moscow. The American

---

* One of these was strategic and logistic, since it had been decided that the British armies would move into Germany in the north, the Americans in the middle and in the south.

secretary of state, the State Department, and Roosevelt himself objected to such reactionary and old-fashioned and imperialist sphere-of-interest arrangements. Churchill argued that these were temporary accommodations, arrangements for the next three months. Stalin — aware and informed of the this disagreement between Roosevelt and Churchill, was canny and clever. At first he was disposed to accept Churchill's proposals, but then advanced the pious argument that the Americans should be consulted. In the end there was no definite agreement, but that Rumania and Bulgaria were principally Russia's business, while Greece was Britain's, amounted to a kind of understanding that went without saying, until October, when Churchill flew to Moscow to nail it down.

◆ ◆ ◆

In August 1944 in Europe the coincidences of great and grave dramatic events presaged the futures of many of its nations. These coincidences, their connections, and their comparable effects were such that I am inclined to describe them, briefly, in the next few pages.

On the first of August started the Warsaw Rising, a most tragic and most courageous episode in the military history of the Second World War. The advancing Russian armies had now come near Warsaw. The underground Polish "Home Army" rose up in Warsaw, driving many of the German occupiers from the center of the city. But the Russians stopped. The Germans came back, with great and brutal force. The Home Army and the people of Warsaw, a city that was now destroyed piecemeal, fought them for sixty-three days, until they were forced to surrender. Stalin refused to help them. Churchill tried, but could not do more than provide a few air drops. Roosevelt was indifferent. What was the meaning of this glaring and ghastly scene of blackening sun and blood? The purpose of these Poles was to liberate their capital city not by the Russians but by themselves—and thus prove to the world their title to it, and to a largely free Poland. Stalin was against anything like that. Churchill could not afford and Roosevelt did not want a break with Stalin about Warsaw. Hitler was still strong; he was firing rockets at London.

It is instructive to look at the destinies of Warsaw and Paris, side by side, in August 1944. The Russian armies were spreading over Poland; they approached Warsaw. The American army began to race across western France; they were approaching Paris. Stalin distrusted independent Poles. He would not give them any place in a Poland to come. Roosevelt disliked and distrusted General de Gaulle and his Free French. He was loath to see them as a government of a France to come. But there the parallel ends. The Russians halted before Warsaw: they let the Poles destroy themselves and let the Germans destroy them. The Americans did not halt before Paris: Eisenhower—after some reluctance—allowed a Free French force, the 2nd French Armored Division, to enter Paris with or even before the first American units. Warsaw was destroyed; Paris remain unscathed. In August 1944 there was more to this than a merely symbolic significance. In August 1944 Warsaw's days and nights were those of blood, sweat, toil, and tears—rivers of blood and many tears; Paris had a few days and nights of unforgettable joy.

Churchill saw what the Russian behavior in Poland meant. He now made what may have been his most determined attempt to forestall what otherwise would amount to a Russian advance into Central Europe. The Allied military plans called for a second invasion of France, now from the south, on France's Mediterranean shore, to take place in mid-August. But the German withdrawal from France was now so rapid that this second invasion was no longer a strategic necessity. Instead, Churchill argued to divert those (Britain and American) forces to northeastern Italy, to advance therefrom into western Yugoslavia, southern Austria, in the direction of Vienna. Roosevelt and Eisenhower would have nothing to do with that. They rejected Churchill's insistent and now often bitter urgings, not only because of their possible military impracticability; they saw in them a political attempt to establish some kind of a British presence in southeastern Europe, a de facto confection of spheres of interest, distasteful to Americans. Otherwise, Churchill's prestige was still considerable. Later in August he went to Italy, where he received the Yugoslavian Communist Tito, who until then had more British than Russian materiel and other support. Bedecking himself in a tight marshal's uniform, looking like a Balkan Göring, Tito, sweating uncomfortably atop his high marshal's collar and gold braids, presented himself to the great British statesman, the liberator of much of Europe. (Soon Tito realized that there would be not British but Russian armies arriving in Yugoslavia. He stopped perspiring and started calculating.) Churchill also saw the pope, Pius XII, who spoke at length about the dangers of Communism, something with which Churchill of course agreed, though much impressed he was not. The problem was not really Communism; it was Russia.

August 1944—for a moment it looked (indeed it was) like September 1918, when Bulgaria and Turkey dropped out of the war and Germany's resolution began to crumble. But 1944 was different. Hitler was not Wilhelm; the Führer was not the Kaiser. In August 1918 in France the last great German offensive had been halted, an Allied counteroffensive had begun; the Germans were now on the defensive, their allies showed signs of deserting them. They were still in the middle of France and Flanders and well inside European Russia, but, for the first time, some of their martinet field marshals concluded that their war was lost. In

August 1944 the Germans were giving up just about all of France and Western Europe west of the Rhine, their cities were destroyed piecemeal by American and British bombing, the Russians were pushing them out of all of Eastern Europe, their allies were deserting them week after week, but they still fought on. Their Führer and their generals knew that they could not win the war, but they were also determined not to lose it; and so they fought, supported by the majority of the German and the German-speaking peoples of Europe, for another nine months, to the Bitter End: a phrase of two words that, to sum up the state of Germany and the Germans in May 1945, was certainly not a cliché. Had the Germans defied Hitler and given up in August 1944, millions of lives could have been spared. But a division of Europe (and of their country) could not have been avoided.

What human dramas were played out in Eastern Europe in August 1944! Early that month Rumania's General Antonescu, a stalwart soldier, favored by Hitler, came to see him. Hitler knew that Antonescu's regime had been attempting to contact the Western Allies, perhaps even Russia; but about that he said nothing to Antonescu (though he dropped a remark about the possibility of a German super-weapon). A fortnight later, the Russians began a great offensive southwestward, into the Balkans, driving into Rumania. Two days later came a revolution in Bucharest, presided over by a young king; in the anteroom of his palace Antonescu was arrested (later to be executed); within twenty-four hours Rumania changed sides. Marshal Mannerheim, the great statesman, creator, and protector of modern Finland, let Hitler know (at least indirectly) that now he had to treat with Stalin, which was what then happened. Bulgaria, moving out of the German camp, was not at war with Russia; but then Stalin thought it best to quickly declare war on Bulgaria and so march into a Sofia unencumbered by a liberal and democratic political leadership. In Hungary closest to Germany, the regent appointed a new prime minister whose — unspoken — task was to prepare that country's surrender to the Allies, including Russia, if must be.

Thus, within a month, the Germans were out of Paris and Brussels and Bucharest and Sofia and Helsinki and soon to be out of Athens too — though not yet of Budapest and Vienna. But the lines of the coming division of Europe became ever more apparent by the day.

◆ ◆ ◆

In October 1944 Churchill flew to Moscow, to meet Stalin alone, for the second time. The first time was August 1942, when he had to tell Stalin about a Second Front: when and how he and the Americans would land in the Mediterranean. Now his agenda consisted of two matters — both about the partition of Europe. One of these matters was the protracted problem of Poland. This was no longer where the frontiers of Poland would be; it was who would rule Poland. That Poland fell within Russia's sphere was not questionable. But what would that mean? a government dominated by Communists entirely, or mostly, or partly? Churchill did not achieve much in that regard. (He took some melancholy satisfaction from seeing how little Stalin thought of his Polish Communist toadies — but then they were *his* puppets, which was what mattered.)

The other matter was more urgent. Churchill put it on the top of his agenda. Impatient by nature, he brought it up with Stalin instantly, in the first hour of their very first evening together. The Russian armies were pouring into the Balkans and into Hungary (which country, rightly, Churchill did not consider as part of the Balkans). There would be no British or American military presence in that part of Europe. Let us agree to divide our responsibilities, Churchill said: both of us have agents in some of these countries; there must be no conflict between them. He put a paper before Stalin. On it he wrote:

Rumania		
	Russia	90%
	The others	10%
Greece		
	Great Britain	90%
	(in accord with U.S.A.)	
	Russia	10%
Yugoslavia		50–50%
Hungary		50–50%
Bulgaria	Russia	75%

Stalin looked at this. With his blue pencil he made a tick on it: all right. "It took less than a minute." There was a moment of silence. Churchill said that this was but a temporary agreement, needed for a few months before the end of the war. Yet both of them knew what it meant: that it was thus that the fate of entire states and peoples had been nailed down by two men, the leaders of two great empires on the edges of Europe. But was there another alternative? Not at all.

There followed some haggling, between their respective foreign ministers. The Russians were now deep within Hungary; and during the very days of Churchill's presence in Moscow a Hungarian attempt to break loose of Hitler and stop fighting the Russians collapsed. In the end Molotov (he was a better haggler than Eden) got 75 percent in Hungary. Churchill was still concerned about Hungary, which to him was a Central European, not a Balkan, state; as late as December he tried to remind Roosevelt of that (and next May President Truman, but by then the Russians had occupied Hungary entirely, though

they had not yet imposed a mostly Communist regime there).*
But Churchill succeeded in what for him was most important.
He saved Greece. Stalin agreed to leave Greece to the British.
(He also forbade Bulgarian and Russian troops to enter northeastern Greece, Thrace, adjacent to Bulgaria.) In Greece a
guerrilla war was developing between Communists and non-
Communists. The Germans retreated from Greece but tried to
foment trouble, letting each side help itself to a few small arms.
By early December the Communist-ruled guerrillas came close to
controlling most of Athens. Churchill decided to send British
forces from Italy to Greece, where they helped to contain and
defeat the Communists and where a national government was
then formed, with Churchill present, who, leaving his family at
home for Christmas, felt compelled to fly to Athens and help in
that government's formation. For this he and the British were
openly, at times violently, attacked by the American press and by
American commentators, and criticized by the State Department
itself.

Stalin said nothing. The Soviet press wrote nothing. One day
in Yalta Stalin gave a friendly wink to Churchill, congratulating
him for having dealt expeditiously in Greece.

◆ ◆ ◆

Before arriving at Yalta we ought to glance, if only for a moment,
at how the Germans (Hitler) and the Americans (Roosevelt)
saw the partition of Europe as it was beginning to take shape.
The story of Hitler and of the Germans was the simpler one,
though not without some significant details. We have seen that

---

* It is noteworthy that when in October Churchill spoke of the desirability
of an eventual Danubian confederation with Vienna at its center (Austria,
Bavaria, Hungary, Württemberg, Baden), Stalin said that he was not inclined to disagree; but without Hungary.

since late 1941 Hitler knew that he could not win *his* war; but he thought that one or the other of his enemies could be forced to deal with him. That would have to be the result of a German military triumph somewhere, on one of the fronts. By 1944 he had not many reasons for such an expectation (though his surprising offensive in the Ardennes in December was meant to achieve that, among other things). More enduring was his belief that the unnatural coalition of his enemies, Anglo-Americans and Russians, would sooner or later break apart. His supporters and some of his remaining allies at times asked him to allow attempts to contact one or another of his enemies for the purpose of eventual negotiation. He, almost always, forbade that, convinced that this would signal a break in Germany's resolution to fight. In early 1945 his foreign minister Ribbentrop asked permission to fly to Moscow; he refused. There were instances when he knew that Heinrich Himmler's people were negotiating with American agents; on one occasion he flew at Himmler about that; on others he seemed to tacitly let him proceed. With the most significant episode of his people negotiating with Americans I shall deal in Chapter 7. What concerns us here is the division of Europe about which Hitler now could do and did little or nothing.

What may be worthy of mention here is the rise of the idea of "Europe," mostly for German propaganda purposes, after Stalingrad. That propaganda, with more or less success, was directed to the Eastern Front: that Germany and her armies were the main bulwarks and defenders of Europe, indeed of Western civilization, against the invasion by brutal and diabolical Asiatics and Russians. There were people, previously indifferent to such "European" ideas, who were inclined to believe this — especially in those parts of Eastern Europe that had been overrun by the Red Army and subjected to Soviet rule before. Many

National Socialists and remaining Fascists in Italy and Western Europe believed it, too; it was largely thus that tens of thousands of young people, from diverse countries of Europe, offered their lives and fought on Hitler's side until the very last days of the war.

Americans, by and large, were not concerned with the division of Europe until much later, well after the end of the war.* However, there were dual tendencies and even dual policies on the highest levels of the United States government. Roosevelt was willing to treat Italy as belonging to the American (and British) sphere of influence. In September 1944 the president and his advisers accepted the so-called Morgenthau Plan proposing the permanent abolition of Germany's industry and the punitive "pastoralization" of Germany—even though this was shelved and abandoned later. At the same time a secret intelligent apparatus, the OSS, set up an office in Bern, Switzerland, where its chief, Allen Dulles, was in contact with many kinds of German personalities, including an SS general, the commander in Italy, with the unspoken purpose to avoid a pro-Russian Germany either near the end or or after the war. In France, too, in August and September 1944 American intelligence agents attempted to ascertain whether Communists in France would or would not become powerful enough to enter the government after liberation. But, again, much of this belongs less to the partition of Europe than among the first scattered signs of the "cold war."

◆ ◆ ◆

* One exception was the Polish-American population, anxious about ancestral land or homeland. Their numbers could—perhaps—influence the outcome of elections in one or two industrial states. Roosevelt was aware of this. He mentioned his concern about this to Stalin, who did not understand that at all—the provincial arithmetic of the American electoral system was unfamiliar to him.

During the sixty years after Yalta something like a generalized consensus has congealed, especially in Europe, suggesting that Yalta amounted to its division. This is a half-truth. The Yalta summit took place in early February 1945. By that time the Russian armies had overrun just about all of Poland and East Prussia (what were left were the sieges of Königsberg and Danzig), also almost all of Hungary and Slovakia; they were less than one hundred miles from Berlin. That was the situation de facto. Still, Poland remained the most difficult subject at Yalta. Many sessions of that longest of the Three-Power summits concerned Poland. Poland was being moved westward; it lost a large portion of its prewar territory (which was, however, inhabited by many non-Polish peoples); it was now given most of East Prussia, much of Pomerania and Upper Silesia, ancient German lands, up to the two rivers of the Oder and Neisse, including even the German port of Stettin. Churchill grumbled about stuffing too much German food into the Polish goose, but in the end he, too, agreed. It was taken for granted that these lands would soon be emptied by their German populations, many of them fleeing westward, while the remaining Germans would be expelled after the end of the war.

Yet the main question remained: not the shape of Poland but its government. Churchill tried to reach a last compromise, some kind of a partial fusion of the democratic and liberal Poles, most of them still in London, with the Communist and pro-Communist Moscow-imposed group now in Warsaw. Stalin would not hear of such a fusion of two Polish governments. He would go so far as to admit some of the democratic Poles to minor posts in Warsaw and to elections in Poland. More than that Churchill could not achieve. It was not much. Roosevelt supported him very desultorily. He, though frail and ill, was much heartened at Yalta because of other agreements he made with Stalin that were of much greater importance for him: they involved the Soviet Union entering the United Nations and Stalin's definite commitment to attack Japan three months after the war in Europe would end. Essentially, Yalta brought about an American-Soviet partition of the Far East — a partition that, unlike that of Europe, then did not last long because of the rise of China. Such is the providential unpredictability of history.

Recall what Stalin said to Eden in December 1941, when the German armies were still before Moscow: "A declaration I regard as algebra, but an agreement as practical arithmetic." Now when his armies were closing in on Berlin, he found that he might — indeed that he would — profit from American algebra, which was the Declaration of Liberated Europe signed at Yalta. The arithmetic was his Percentages' Agreement with Churchill.* To many people, especially Americans, Yalta looked like a general agreement, including Stalin's acceptance, for free democratic elections everywhere in Europe. To Stalin it meant something quite different: a tacit American acceptance of the partition of Europe. "What is ours is ours; what is theirs is theirs," he said to a visiting Yugoslav Communist a few months later. In a message to Churchill shortly before Hitler's suicide, Stalin wrote: "The question of Poland is for the security of the Soviet Union what the question of Belgium and Greece is for the security of Great Britain."

◆ ◆ ◆

Less than two weeks after Yalta Stalin manifested his interpretation of the Declaration of Liberated Europe. His minion Vishinsky descended suddenly on Bucharest, where he demanded

---

* One exception to that was Yugoslavia: by February 1945 no longer 50–50 but predominantly pro-Communist and pro-Russian. (An inconclusive agreement about Yugoslavia's government was also formulated at Yalta.)

and brutally enforced a transformation of the Rumanian government. The British were shocked, but they thought they could not do much, since the Percentages' Agreement had largely allotted Rumania to the Russians. The Russians' behavior in Poland suggested nothing resembling a compromise. The American government and public opinion still clung to the notion that in the countries of Europe occupied by the Russian armies, the Russian sphere of interest together with more or less "free" elections meant the establishment of pro-Russian but not necessarily Communist regimes. Churchill thought otherwise. For him the essential and now more and more urgent question was: where will the British and American and Russian armies meet? Whereto will the Russian armies advance? By the end of March the Russians were approaching Vienna but not yet Prague and Berlin. And now the weakening of German armed forces in the west was such that at last the armies of the Western powers were moving across Germany much faster than were the Russians. Stalin was beginning to worry about that. He had not much reason to. At the end of March General Eisenhower, without advising Churchill, sent a message to Stalin informing him that the American armies would not aim at Berlin or Prague — which indeed they did not.

Meanwhile, great news of great events gathered from 12 April to 9 May. President Roosevelt died; Russian and American troops met in the middle of Germany; Hitler killed himself; the Germans surrendered; the Russians conquered Berlin and marched into Prague. Churchill now thought that there was a last chance to mitigate the partition of Europe — more precisely: to mitigate the conditions of half of Europe's subservience to Russia. He thought that the United States and Britain had one important card to play. This was the fact that the American (and in a few places the British) armies had met the Russians in places well within the Russian occupation zone established a year before by the tripartite

European Advisory Commission. Perhaps an American and British withdrawal to their designated occupation zones could be made contingent on Moscow's willingness to be more moderate about Poland. But Washington would not agree to anything like that. Also there was, as yet, no American or British presence in the Central European capitals conquered by the Russians, Berlin and Vienna. But just before 1 July the American armies in central Germany began to withdraw to their occupation zones, and on 1 July the first American and British troops were permitted to enter Berlin and Vienna to occupy the zones allotted to them two years before by the European Advisory Commission. It was on 1 July, too, that London and Washington announced their official recognition of the Warsaw Polish government.

There followed the Potsdam Conference, the last grand summit of the Second World War, with Stalin, Churchill, and the new American president, Truman. Its deliberations and agreements did little or nothing about the partition of Europe or even about Germany — except that a preliminary agreement about which power would gather and collect German material goods, "reparations" — which was the first symptom of a tacit acceptance of dividing Germany along the zonal occupation boundaries. There was hardly any discussion about the political future of Germany. Stalin showed no interest in Austria beyond the Russian occupation zones (in Austria the Russians had permitted the installation of a Socialist-led but not pro-Communist government); he did not seem insistent, at least not yet, on the Communization of Czechoslovakia or even of Hungary. Nor did he advance the actual frontiers of the Soviet Union unduly. He had added to them a few segments of eastern Finland, a large portion of prewar eastern Poland, the former tsarist province of Bessarabia from Rumania in 1944, the province of Transcarpathian Ukraine granted him by the Czechoslovak government in 1945, and — the only novelty in Russia's political geography — the Königsberg enclave. All in all, the Soviet Union in Europe now comprised less than did Tsarist Russia a century earlier (when, for instance, most of Poland and all of Finland had been provinces within the Russian state). But now conditions were different. Beyond the confines of the tsar's empire there had existed no Russian sphere of interest. What now did this "sphere of interest" mean?

In this respect let us follow the history of the phrase *Iron Curtain*. This designation first appeared in 1921, referring to the rigid closing of the frontiers of the Communist Soviet Union, hermetically separating it from its neighbors and from the rest of Europe. (Note that this was not the case of France after the French Revolution.) In February 1945 Goebbels resurrected this phrase in an article. If the Russians won, he wrote, then behind an iron curtain the murder of masses of people would occur, while in the rest of Western Europe its Bolshevization would inevitably proceed. It is doubtful that Churchill read or was informed about Goebbels's article. Perhaps the 1921 phrase may have lived in his mind. He used the term first in a poignant letter to President Truman on 12 May 1945.* The text of his message is significant, because he went to considerable extent about the historic importance of Poland, Czechoslovakia, Hungary, and Austria (though not Rumania and Bulgaria, which were in Russia's sphere not only due to the Percentages' Agreement but because of their proximity and their historical ties to Russia). Yet his employing the phrase *Iron Curtain* was more than a stylistic choice. He said that the West was now being cut off from a large portion not only of Eastern but of Central Europe. President

---

*On 30 May he drafted another long telegram to the president that in the end he decided not to send.

Truman was less optimistic about Stalin and the Russians than his predecessor had been. But he was, as yet, no more inclined to agree to Churchill's anxious proposals than had been Roosevelt; and by the time he and his government chose to confront the Russians here or there, much of the partition of Europe had become an accomplished fact. Meanwhile, Churchill, too, was out of his office as prime minister of Britain, since the Conservatives had lost the British general election in late July 1945.

The end of the Second World War, with the surrender of Japan, came but two weeks later: but since the subject of this chapter is the division of Europe, I am compelled to carry the story of its development a little farther. *Iron Curtain* became a current phrase only in and after March 1946 — because of Churchill's famous Iron Curtain speech in Fulton, Missouri. He had come to the United States as a private citizen, guest of President Truman; but that speech became one of his most celebrated ones. What he said was essentially what he had written to Truman ten months before. His concern was the establishment of police states in Eastern Europe and the consequent division of Europe into two. He spoke of an Iron Curtain descending from Stettin on the Baltic to Trieste on the Adriatic. (He did not yet include eastern Germany — that is, the Russian occupation zone in Germany — in a Europe imprisoned beyond the Iron Curtain.)

There is a matter that we must consider. The history of the division of Europe and that of Germany was not the same. Within the division of Europe there was the division of Germany, and within Germany the division of Berlin: but the status of Germany was still a subject of discussions between the Western Allies and the Soviet foreign minister as late as 1947, though without any results. By 1949 the partition of Germany had crystallized. Evidently there was a western, democratic German state, made up by the American, British, and French occupation zones and also their zones in Berlin — while in East Germany a "German Democratic Republic" came to exist, with its own government, encompassing the Russian occupation zone and the Russian sector of Berlin. After the failure of his attempt to blockade West Berlin, in 1949 Stalin and his successors thought it best not to force the Western Powers out of Berlin, whose partition was not wholly complete (while at the same time mine fields, barbed-wire fences, and an almost complete hermetic isolation from the West of the states behind the Iron Curtain was established). Through the not entirely complete segregation of East from West Berlin, millions of East Germans were seeping through, moving to the west, until in September 1961 the East German government (with somewhat reluctant agreement from Moscow) chose to erect a monstrous wall, separating the two Berlins — at the very time where elsewhere the Iron Curtain separating this or that Eastern European state from the West began to leak, loosen, corrode. But the end of the division of Berlin and of Germany and of Europe then occurred together, with the end of the cold war, in 1989.

FOUR

Hitler, Questions Still Extant

Hitler was not simple. The popular attribution of his character and of his life is that of a narrow-minded fanatic: but this is incorrect, imprecise, and insufficient. He was hate-filled, rather than narrow-minded: two inclinations that are not the same (for one thing, hate sharpens the mind, while narrow-mindedness obscures and limits it). Categorizing him as mad, or even psychotic, absolves him of responsibility for what he did and ordered and said. It absolves us, too, from thinking about him, by sweeping the Hitler problem under the rug. This will not do. There are still prevalent (and debatable) questions about Hitler. However, in this book my scope is necessarily limited: questions not about Adolf Hitler in extenso but questions about Hitler in the Second World War.

This encompasses less than six years, and the last six years of his life. In the majority of Hitler's biographies the space devoted to those six years is small. In the case of his German biographers this may be understandable. Whatever Hitler may have done in Germany, the world war that he began was his and Germany's undoing. But then, after all, he (and his Germany) did come close to winning the war: his war.

His war. That alone qualifies him for having been the most extraordinary figure in the history of the twentieth century. No Hitler, no Second World War — certainly not the one that began in September 1939. He was the *only* leader who wanted a war then: a war against Poland *if* Poland would not accept his demands;* and a war even if the British and the French would keep their word to Poland and declare war against Germany. (They declared the war and were then reluctant to fight it: but that is another story.)

The war that began in September 1939 was Hitler's war: but we must at least question the accepted opinion that he wanted war all along. Yes, he wanted to conquer much of Eastern Europe and perhaps much of European Russia too, through war, if need be. He believed that force, many kinds of force, made history; that (reversing Clausewitz) politics was like war, though with other means. But he did not want a *world* war; he did not want a war against Britain, or one against the United States (or perhaps not even against Russia, at least not in 1939). Contrary to those who thought and wrote that he planned a world war in stages — as Andreas Hillgruber's *Stufenplan:* a war for Eastern Europe, and then one in Western Europe, and then against Britain, and then against Russia, and, later, one against the United States — are wrong. That is what eventually happened; but it was not what he wanted. He made two miscalculations — or, rather, he

* His demands were nothing less than to make Poland subservient, at best a junior partner of Germany, a state without an independent foreign policy. The British historian A. J. P. Taylor's statement, "Only Danzig prevented cooperation between Germany and Poland," is entirely wrong.

had two hopes — that were fatal for him. In 1940 he hoped that after his conquest of Western Europe the British would accept his domination of Europe while he would not insist on the demolition of the British Empire. In 1941 he hoped that after his conquest of Soviet Russia, Britain and the United States would have to accept the hopelessness of continuing a war against him. In both cases he failed: but not by much.

There was a personal, and deeper, reason for his failure. This was his timing. Some time in 1938 — which was his most successful year — he seems to have convinced himself (against some physical evidence) that he would not live long; that therefore he must not let matters wait; that time was working against him and against Germany; that its now achieved military and political superiority would diminish because the Western democracies, even though reluctantly, were beginning to rearm. Shortly before the start of the war in August 1939, his ally Mussolini wrote him that this was not so, that time was not favoring their adversaries. But Hitler did not listen: and the result was a second world war.

He declenched it; but not only did he come close to winning it; it took almost six years for the greatest powers of the world to defeat him and his Germany. That alone makes him the most extraordinary figure in the history of an entire century; and that alone, despite the undoubtable record of his criminal intentions and decisions may, I am afraid, contribute — we must hope that only in some ways and only in the minds and hearts of some people — to some kind of a recrudescence of his reputation as the twenty-first century proceeds.

There are fresh flowers some people put, almost every week, on his parents' regilded gravestone in the cemetery of Leonding, Austria. There is a well-worn path leading to it, more than one hundred years after their deaths and more than sixty years after the death of their son.

◆ ◆ ◆

The lately fashionable comparisons of Hitler with Stalin — which of them murdered or ordered the murders of more people — are senseless. Hitler came to be the accepted leader of the then perhaps most educated people of the world; Stalin of one of the least educated people of the white race. More than a half-century after their deaths there are no admirers of Stalin who are not Russians (or Georgians); but there are still many admirers of Hitler who are not Germans or Austrians.

However — their lives had one thing in common. At some time in his career each discovered his talents for statesmanship. To trace this mutation is easier in Stalin's life than in Hitler's. It came in the 1930s, with Stalin's realization of the superior importance of state and of nation compared with class and to ideology. The evidence is there in many of his decisions but also in some of his statements.* Hitler — whose main talent was his uncanny (and often sinister) insight into human nature — realized very early in his political career that the relations of states were not really different from the relations of individual persons. There are noteworthy evidences of his talent for statesmanship, of his at times astonishing successes (but also of sometimes less astonishing mistakes) in his management of Germany's relations with other states before 1939.

And then his capacity for statesmanship — not at all independent of his ability as a strategist and war leader — went on during the war. His talents carried him far, but not far enough. The still

---

* Cf. my *June 1941: Hitler and Stalin,* especially pp. 47–56.

largely accepted view (especially among Germans) that, whatever his military talents, he was devoid of an elementary understanding of statesmanship, is wrong: because at the summit of events, of military and political events, the uses (and abuses) of force are almost always the same.

That he knew very well. What he did not understand — and this was one of the greatest shortcomings of his mind — was that his adversaries, no matter how disparate, were bound together by one, perhaps only one, dominant conviction: that in this war he and his Germany must be conquered, unconditionally so; that no peace or armistice must be made or even imagined with him.* Well before his demise he predicted that the unnatural coalition between the United States and Britain and the Soviet Union would break apart. And the Russian-British-American alliance did break apart; but without him, and too late for him. He was solely responsible for starting the Second World War; but he was also responsible for its lasting so long, and for the horrors before its end.

But: what he had to do, and did, during the war was to balance and weigh his ideology with statesmanship: his idealism with his realism; his fanaticism with caution. And before I get to some of the examples of this duality one last remark about his person and character: we must recognize his penchant for secrecy. On several instances he felt compelled to speak about his secrecy to officials dependent on his decisions.† This goes contrary to the accepted opinion that he was an often incessant

---

* Napoleon, too, believed in 1814 that one victory in the field could change the course of events. But here is the difference: as late as March 1814 the victorious Allies were willing to discuss peace terms with Napoleon (for example at the conference of Châtillon). But not with Hitler.

† Hitler to Admiral Raeder on 23 May 1939: he possesses three kinds of secrecy, "the first, when we talk among ourselves; the second, I keep for myself; the third, these are problems about the future of which I keep thinking [die ich nicht zu Ende denke]."

talker; or that his entire view of the world and many of his consequent decisions may be found in *Mein Kampf* and in other statements of his, either early or later in his career. He certainly possessed the talent to convince people, sometimes astonishingly so, even in the face of contrary evidences; he knew how to employ this talent, not only in public speeches but also when speaking to all kinds of officials, to all kinds of his minions, even in his recorded table conversations, in which his statements and phrases were ever so often meant to impress his hearers—while those phrases or statements were not always incontrovertible evidences of what he really thought.*

Yet it is not impossible to piece together evidences of what Hitler really thought and wanted throughout the war. And many of these evidences suggest differences perhaps not so much between what he said and what he thought but between his ideology and his statesmanship: evidences of the, so often inescapable, duality of his mind.

◆ ◆ ◆

One of the mysteries that, I fear, we shall never be able to answer or solve, is his hesitation before Dunkirk. He ordered the halt of one of his armies moving from the south toward Dunkirk when they could have penetrated the still largely unassembled lines of defense in a day or so. Moreover: even after he lifted his halt order after two days, the advance of another mass of German troops, moving toward Dunkirk from the west, was slow. After a week, then, 339,000 British and French soldiers, while abandoning all of their equipment, were able to be shipped back to

---

* In this, too, he was the opposite of his great adversary Churchill, who was a believer in the written, rather than in the spoken, word; who kept few secrets, and was inclined to speculate aloud about many things that sprang from or flitted through his sprightly mind.

England. We cannot know what would have happened if Hitler's armies would have captured them. We do know that Dunkirk lifted the morale of the British (though not of the French) people, and that it immeasurably strengthened Churchill's hand. But: what were Hitler's motives? About his purposes we can say something that is not only plausible but of which the evidence is there in many of his words: he hoped that the British, whether forced to do so or not, would accept his domination of Europe (and their subsequent, and at least partial, dependence on his power and goodwill). But purposes and motives are not the same. What were his motives in the halt order? Before Dunkirk he said that he did not want to destroy the British Empire, from which Germany would profit less than Japan and the United States. After Dunkirk, and especially in his last reported statements in the spring of 1945, he said that he had given the British "a sporting chance" at the time of Dunkirk, "a golden bridge," and that he thus let the hundreds of thousands of British troops there go. He said this before his ultimate defeat and death; we ought to discount it as we know of his purpose of saying some things to the circle of his closest intimates. Still the motive of the halt order of 24 May 1940 (sent also in clear, which the British could immediately read), as well as the subsequent lack of an order for a fierce and unconditional push into Dunkirk, remain at least questionable.

One plausible explanation, supported by evidence, is that at that very time Hitler had become hesitant, whence his caution. He hardly believed his good luck. The speed of the German army's advance across northern France and Belgium astonished the world, and it astonished him too. Around 20 May, about ten days after the start of the German offensive across Western Europe, he, at times, uttered words of amazement and of caution, fearing, among other things, an Allied counteroffensive cutting off the advancing armored snout of the German army. That was certainly one of the reasons behind his halt order. There was another reason, again military rather than political. Göring told him, days before Dunkirk, that the Luftwaffe would make any British attempt of evacuation from Dunkirk catastrophic, if not impossible. To the dismay of some of his generals, Hitler went along with this, but then Göring's promise did not quite come about. And perhaps here our questioning must halt, too. After all, monocausal explanations of motives and purposes often may be at best close but seldom very close to truth. Neither motives nor purposes are simple. We may content ourselves by stating that Hitler's motives (rather than his purposes) in the Dunkirk halt order were a mixture of military caution and political calculation.

The consequences of Dunkirk were great; indeed, decisive for the eventual outcome of the Second World War. They had two effects on Hitler. One was his now increased and increasing hatred for Britain and the British. That issued from a deep-seated flaw of his character, observable early in his career: his hatred for men and people who opposed him, who stood athwart his plans. In and after September 1939 his hatred for Poles rose above whatever respect he may have had for them: because they had chosen to resist him and thus declench the Second World War. After the summer of 1940 his hatred for the British grew into something much greater than whatever consideration he had had for them before. There are many examples of this, including his hatred for Churchill, deeper than any hatred for Stalin or even for Roosevelt. In 1940 he was uncertain about the potential success of a German invasion of Britain across the Channel; he was uncertain, too (indeed, even before the beginning), of Göring's plan to force the British to their knees by aerial warfare. The result was Hitler's decision to deprive Britain of its last possible hope and potential ally in Europe. He would invade and conquer Russia, whereafter he would be invincible in Europe, whence Churchill (and his new ally Roosevelt) would be compelled to give up warring against him.

It is widely thought that Hitler's two greatest mistakes were his declarations of war against Russia and against the United States in 1941. About the former: there was method to his madness, if madness that was. His decision to conquer European Russia included his desire to secure vast lands for his great German empire and its people. But again his purposes were not simple or monocausal. His immediate and main reason in 1941 was to deprive Britain of a last hope on the European continent. There are many evidences of this. About his declaration of war on the United States in December 1941: he was obliged by his alliance with Japan to do so; more important, the United States was already involved in a naval war against Germany in the Atlantic many months before December 1941.* The question, therefore, is not why Hitler declared war on Russia and on the United States: these questions have been discussed, back and forth, and given various interpretations during the past sixty years; and at least serious scholars will agree that in 1941 he had tried to conquer Russia and also to avoid a definite war with the United States, and that in December 1941 he failed. The question, for the purposes of this book, is this: Did he understand what this meant—and when? Did he know that he could no longer win the Second World War? An overall answer to these

---

* This is why on the day before his declaration of war on Russia (on 21 June 1941), he gave a peremptory order to all German naval craft in the Atlantic: avoid firing at American vessels in any circumstance, even in defense (for of course that would play into Roosevelt's hands). This connection between his Russian and American plans was very important.

questions was made by General Alfred Jodl during his imprisonment in Nuremberg. Jodl, who knew Hitler well, who was close to him, and who was one of the few who would not deny him or even mitigate his respect for him, wrote in a letter dictated to his wife from his prison: Hitler's "military advisers — today one often hears it said — should certainly have made it clear to him that the war was lost. What a naive thought! Earlier than any person in the world, Hitler sensed and knew that the war was lost. But can one give up a Reich and a people before they are lost? A man like Hitler could not do it." In another statement Jodl said that by the winter of 1941 Hitler knew that "victory [could] no longer be achieved."*

All of this meant and means more than an answer to a historian's chronological curiosity: when? What followed was the Russians pushing the Germans back before Moscow and the American entry into the war. But we must understand that Hitler's realization of this meant not an admission of defeat but an almost instant, and nearly complete, transformation of his war strategy. Hitler recognized that he could no longer win *his* war; but that he could sustain, or even win, a different war. He could no longer win the war that he had begun, but that did not mean that he would, or must, lose it. From that moment in December 1941 on, Hitler's strategy aimed at disrupting the unnatural coalition of his enemies, a political aim that must be achieved by

* As cited on page 31, which I feel compelled to repeat here: Hitler on 18 November 1941: "The recognition, by both opposing coalitions, that they cannot annihilate each other leads to a negotiated peace." Also: "We must consider the possibility that it will not be possible for either of the principal opponents to annihilate the other, or to subdue them entirely." Note that Hitler said these things even *before* the last lunge of the German Army Group Center toward Moscow.

military means. He was convinced of the supreme importance of force: when one or another of his minions or generals suggested a political approach to one or another of his enemies, he invariably answered that this could not and must not happen before a military victory on one front or another, an impressive blow. We shall see that, sometimes grudgingly, he allowed one or two political moves (significant rather than important ones). But over all of that stood his determination, congealing by December 1941, to keep his Germany sufficiently powerful, rock-hard enough for at least one of its enemies to fail against it. Now his great model was not Bismarck but Frederick the Great, not the statesman who had united Germany and made it the most powerful state in Europe but the king who had defied his enemies, defeating them here or there, until the overwhelming (and unusual) coalition of his enemies broke apart and his Prussia emerged as one of the winners. In sum: after a series of short wars Germany must be made ready for a long war.*

This mutation of Hitler's political strategy required a massive transformation of the German economy and industry. A change from a partial war economy to a more or less total one was decreed by Hitler in early 1942, when, among other things, he named Albert Speer the director of the German war economy after Fritz Todt perished in an air accident. (The phrase *total war* was invoked by Goebbels to an enthusiastic audience one year

---

*Thus, while 1939–1941 was the phase of great German offensives, November 1942–April 1945 was that of protracted German defensives (interrupted by German counteroffensives on occasion) — contrary to the still accepted view that till the very end Hitler refused to allow his armies to retreat. (Consider, too, that while it took the Germans five months in 1941 to get close to Moscow, and sixteen months in 1941–1942 to reach Stalingrad, it took the Russians two and a half years to drive the Germans back to Vienna and Berlin.)

later, after the military catastrophe of Stalingrad.) There was another mutation, or change in plans, in January 1942. This was the decision to change the policy of expulsion from Germany (and of ghettoization in Poland) to one collection of all the remaining Jews from Germany and Europe, eventually with the result of their extermination. It may or may not be a coincidence that the conference of experts summoned to decide this had been originally set for 8 December 1941 (the day after America's entry into the war) and then postponed to 22 January 1942, meeting in the Berlin suburb of Wannsee.

◆ ◆ ◆

I must turn — alas, ever so briefly — to the question of Hitler and Jews, a question that includes but also transcends the history of the Second World War. Yet relevant to the scope of the war the question remains: what did he really think? This question is not identical with "did he say what he meant?" because — and there are many evidences of this — ever so often his mind was carried away by his very words when he spoke: that is, he did not feign sincerity or conviction for rhetorical purposes; on many occasions he believed what he was saying while he was saying it. Should we rest content with the widely, almost universally, accepted view that a hatred for and fear of Jews was his main conviction, dominant over just about everything else? There exists ample evidence for such a view, including the decision to proceed from the expulsion and sequestration of Jews to their mass extermination. But there is much evidence, too, for another of his inclinations: to employ anti-Semitism for rhetorical and political purposes. He learned early in his life that anti-Semitism in Austria and Germany was potentially popular; and then also that it is useful to identify for the masses a tangible, a particular, actual and potential incarnation of evil. These two inclinations were of course allied. But were they identical?

We know, from many sources, including Hitler's own auto-historical *Mein Kampf,* that during his formative years in Vienna he was much impressed with the popularity of Mayor Karl Lueger, who won his election with the help of his anti-Semitic rhetoric. Another, even more radically anti-Semitic, political figure at the time was Georg von Schönerer, who — unlike Lueger — campaigned for Austria to become a part of the German Reich. Hitler's nationalism was much like Schönerer's; yet he was much more impressed with Lueger than with Schönerer, whose popularity was minimal and marginal compared with Lueger's. We must also consider that Lueger's anti-Semitism was much less drastic than Schönerer's, and after he assumed the office of mayor of Vienna (at first he had been opposed by the Emperor Franz Josef), his radical anti-Semitism relented and well nigh disappeared.

During Hitler's formative years in Vienna, and during the no less formative years as a soldier, we have few evidences of anything more than a then common, and hardly obsessive, kind of anti-Semitism. We know that the sudden and great change in his life came at the relatively advanced age of thirty, in 1919 in Munich after the First World War; that this occurred together with his discovery of his talents as a public speaker; and with the extreme anti-Semitic contents of his rhetoric then and ever after. Evidences of his radical anti-Semitism are then endless, and the subject of entire libraries of articles and books. We also know that after his assumption of power in 1933 (including in some of his instructions for the Nuremberg Laws in 1935), there were instances when he made exceptions, exempting a few German half-

Jews from the severe laws imposed on Jews in Germany.* Of course, these few exceptions were unimportant and insignificant in view of the massive humiliation and mistreatment imposed on the Jews of Germany. More significant is that he publicly declared in January 1939 — that is, before the beginning of the Second World War — that if a war against Germany came about, it would be at least largely the work of international Jews, and that the Jews of Europe would pay a very bitter price for that. There is no reason to think that he said this only for rhetorical purposes. War came; and as it proceeded the expulsion of Jews from Europe was no longer a possible option. Some time around 1941 the German policy of the expulsion or ghettoization of Jews changed to plans for their extermination. There exists no written or oral evidence for a Hitler order to that effect; but the absence of such documentary evidence amounts to nothing more than a politic caution. There is no evidence that Hitler opposed or even that he was left ignorant of the treatment now meted out on the remnant millions of Jews in Germany and in Europe and in the conquered portions of the Soviet Union.

But there is evidence — fragmentary but not insignificant — that even during the Second World War, Hitler's Judaeophobia (in my opinion, at least, a more accurate term than anti-Semitism) was not a simple matter. There are three considerations concerning this.

The first (in order, though not in importance) is Hitler's lack of interest, if not unwillingness to be informed about, the developing extermination of Jews. In his few public speeches after

---

* And even a few Jewish scientists. See Rüdiger Hachtmann, "Die Kaiser-Wilhelm-Gesellschaft 1933 bis 1945," p. 51, in *Vierteljahrshefte für Zeitgeschichte,* January 2008.

1941, and in his many recorded ramblings before various listeners, he made statement after statement about the severe treatment to be expected by Jews, hard conditions that they amply deserved: yet nothing about their physical extermination. More significant: when on at least one occasion (in 1943) Himmler had a precise statistical report of the progress of extermination prepared for and presented to Hitler (and specifically typed for him on Hitler's large-type typewriters), he pushed the paper aside; he was not interested. An explanation of this may accord with an inclination of his, for which we have evidences during the war: his unwillingness to see certain unpleasant things. Thus, for instance, he refused to visit or even to see pictures of the bomb-damaged cities of Germany (even as he spoke, in many instances, of the German revenge — the rockets — to be meted out on Britain, and also of the building of new modern German cities after the war).

The second, and more telling, instance of a difference between his public statements and his own views is extant in his speeches referring constantly to the dangers and evils of "Jewish Bolshevism" (one as late as 16 April 1945) — when we know, from other expressions of his regarding Stalin, that he had a considerable respect for Stalin (among other things because of his anti-Semitism). Hitler did not seriously believe that Stalin's government was ridden with or manipulated by Jews.

The third, and fragmentary, evidence of exceptions to Hitler's categorical decision to exterminate all Jews in Europe resides in the few instances when he, tacitly or otherwise, allowed Himmler to arrange exceptions for Jews in some cases, permitting their departure to neutral countries. Of course this happened almost always when such an exception seemed advantageous to Germany, financially but also politically—in the latter case sowing seeds of distrust among his adversaries.*

In July 1944, after Hungary's Jews had been deported—most of them to Auschwitz—the regent of Hungary ordered the end of deportation of Jews from Budapest. Hitler no longer interfered. In August, Himmler ordered his subordinates not to insist on further deportations from Hungary. In September, Himmler's top aides negotiated with Americans in Switzerland. In October he ordered a stop to the gassings in Auschwitz. (Of course, many thousands still died there after that because of their barbarous mistreatment.) In January 1945 Himmler forbade the destruction of the ghetto in Budapest and the killing of its inhabitants. Did Himmler do these things in order to defy Hitler? He did not.

In any event it should be noted that some of Hitler's statements during the war were contrary to the accepted view of his racism. Both before and during the war he made remarkable statements contrary to the racial doctrine of National Socialist philosophy. There *was* a racist element in his thinking: but he was a populist rather than a racist. "There was and remains," I wrote more than ten years ago, "a superficially slight but essentially

---

*The most telling instances of this took place in Hungary in 1944. One involves Raoul Wallenberg, who was not even a Swedish diplomat but who arrived in Budapest because of his humanitarian convictions and with the help of Jewish and American organizations. The German authorities allowed him to travel through Germany and then stay in Budapest, where they treated him as if he were a representative of American interests (which in some ways he was)—for several reasons, including the Germans' wish to have relations with Americans, and to let the Russians know that. This may have been the main reason for the Russians' arrest of Wallenberg immediately after their occupation of (the Pest side) of Budapest, and of his deportation to Moscow.

profound difference between a *folkish* and a *racist* type of thinking. The response that Hitler wished to evoke was a result of the former rather than the latter. And that reflected, too, the evolution—if that was what it was, it not a gradually hardening recognition—of his own beliefs."* In May 1944, in a speech to officers in the Platterhof, Hitler said: "We have this people of ours that is not to be identified with a race. . . . But when I began [speaking] about twenty-five years ago this was not so. I was told . . . that *Volk* and *Race* are one and the same! No! Volk and race are not the same. Race is a component of blood, a hematological kernel, but the Volk is very often compounded not of one race but of two, three, four, or five different racial kernels. . . . Each of these racial kernels possesses particular talents." And on 14 February 1945 Hitler said to his attentive circle: "Pride of race is a quality which the German, fundamentally, does not possess. We use the term of Jewish race as a matter of convenience, for in reality and from the genetic point of view *there is no such thing as the Jewish race*." These italics are mine.

◆ ◆ ◆

After 1941–1942 Hitler thought and said that the alliance of Germany's enemies must split; it would split; his efforts must be directed to that; and then one or the other of his enemies would be forced to offer him acceptable conditions, and perhaps even an alliance. These were calculations of a statesman—of sorts—and not those of a fanatical ideologue. Thus he spoke, in 1943 and after, to those who ventured to address him with questions or with suggestions that a political solution to the ever growing dangers of the war for Germany must be found. But he invariably answered that such a change must be preceded, indeed be forced

* *The Hitler of History,* pp. 122–123.

out, by a resounding German military victory on one front or another. Otherwise none of his opponents would consider dealing with him. In this he was probably right. We have evidence, too — at times from his own words — that after 1942 some of the desperate German offensives that he himself planned and ordered, such as at Kursk in July 1943 and in Belgium in December 1944, were meant with ultimate political purposes in mind. Whether the expense of offensives in view of the remnant power of his armies was militarily reasonable or wasteful is not our concern here. What we must consider is that, for once, the hopes of most of the German people, spoken or unspoken, were largely in accord with his: that Germany's ultimate hope was a break-up of the alliance of their enemies; and that among their enemies the Americans would be the least revengeful and potentially the most accommodating ones.*

Which is what happened. But that no longer belongs to the history of the Second World War, save for some of its early symptoms toward the end of it. What belongs here is a last summing-up of Hitler's duality, that is, the more than occasional discrepancy between his ideology and his statesmanship, during the war.

For Hitler conquest or, in other words, submission to his wishes, almost always meant vassalage. Within Germany he accepted the support of men who were not National Socialists but "conservatives," who did not oppose him or who were unwilling to act in accord with how he saw his and Germany's interests — especially in foreign policy. He gave them official positions, in the 1930s for some of them, throughout the war for others: Neurath, Schacht, Papen, Weizsaecker. During the war we have innumerable examples of his priorities. National Socialism had

* This is more fully described on pages 171–174.

its adherents in every country of Europe, men and women who were willing and often ambitious and eager to serve as Germany's prime and principal allies. Yet—and this was the case even for some National Socialists in Austria and, after that, in Denmark, Norway, Holland, Belgium, indeed, in just about every country under his sway, such people were disappointed, since Hitler did not entrust them with the government of their countries. In France, too, he preferred to use the Pétain government in Vichy rather than some of the committed French National Socialists in Paris. Even in Norway, where he had a true supporter, Vidkun Quisling, whose loyalty to him and to Germany could not be ascribed to opportunism, Hitler did not let him have an official position until later in the war. A prime example of his priorities was that of Rumania. The government (and also the people) of that country quickly committed themselves to Germany's predominance at the moment of the downfall of France; furthermore, there was a popular and powerful, rabidly anti-Semitic and pro-Hitler National Socialist movement within Rumania, the so-called Iron Guard, the most popular and powerful such group in any country of Europe outside of Germany. In September 1940 a revolution in Rumania forced the king (Carol II) to abdicate and flee; an impressive military man, Antonescu, came to be the leader ("conducator") of the country, supported by the Iron Guard. Hitler met Antonescu a few months later; he was considerably impressed by him. A few months later (in January 1941) the Iron Guard and its ruffians, unsatisfied with their share of power and government, revolted against the Antonescu regime, with the result of three days of bloody civil war in Bucharest. The Iron Guard was beaten down—with German support to the government, including tanks and other armor. Hitler helped and sustained Antonescu unreservedly. A few leaders of the Iron Guard fled — to Germany, where they were sequestrated (or, perhaps, kept in reserve) by Himmler and the SS.

Hitler's reasoning had its simple logic. He and his Germany — for both political and economic reasons — needed order and quiet in states now allied to him.* He gave little or no support to National Socialists beyond Germany. (Within Germany, too, he chose to suspend some of the regulations constraining the Catholic Church, at times against the inclinations of National Socialist chieftains.) He kept to this policy for a long time. He knew that the Horthy regime in Hungary, the regime of Tsar Boris III in Bulgaria, and even Antonescu in Rumania began to extend cautious feelers to the British and the Americans as early as late 1942, preparing to loosen their ties to the Third Reich, perhaps eventually to drop them. These governments also began a tacit lessening of the suppression of Jews in their countries. In the case of Hungary, the relatively most independent of the so-called satellites, Hitler waited long: he did not choose to force a drastic change in Hungary's government and to occupy that country until March 1944. In the case of Rumania he had a last conversation with his favorite, Antonescu, who came to visit him in early August 1944, not more than a fortnight before Rumania

---

* One example of his cautious "statesmanship" (my quotation marks are not accidental): By early 1944 his foreign minister Ribbentrop was exasperated by the moves of Franco's Spain toward "neutrality," with a few steps meant to appease the Western Allies. He drafted an angry note to Madrid. Hitler forbade that. "At this point Hitler intervened personally, realizing that the Spanish regime still expressed friendship [to Germany] and that it was in Germany's best interest to salvage as much as possible of the relationship. On 10 May he issued instructions to Ribbentrop to maintain the best relations possible." Stanley G. Payne, *Franco and Hitler: Spain, Germany, and World War II* (New Haven, 2008), p. 251.

switched sides and Antonescu himself was overthrown and arrested. Hitler knew that men in Antonescu's government had already attempted to contact the British and the Americans. Yet he did not berate Antonescu.

He must have had some understanding of what is involved when in the mind of a nation's leader the immediate interests of his country become urgent and acute. Consider the relative — very relative — moderation of the retribution with which he allowed to live some of those foreign heads of states, recent allies of his who, for the sake of their nations, had decided to break away from Germany in 1944. He kept silent about Marshal Mannerheim of Finland. Horthy, the regent of Hungary, whose armistice attempt Hitler's shock troops brutally smashed, who was arrested by them and then transported to southern Germany with his family, was interned in a castle under relatively — I repeat, relatively — acceptable conditions. Even about the German conspirators who tried to kill him on 20 July 1944 he expressed his contempt for their "ineptitude," perhaps even more than for their treachery. Had they succeeded, what did they expect to do? On one occasion he said to General Bodenschatz: "I know that Stauffenberg, Goerdeler, and Witzleben thought to save the people through my death . . . but these people had absolutely no clear plan what to do then."

His clear plan was to fight to the end and thereby precipitate the inevitable break-up of the alliance of his enemies. Yet beyond and beneath that iron-willed resolution there were instances, especially during the last year of the war, when he, tacitly or otherwise, allowed a few attempts of indirect or even direct contact, especially with his American adversaries. There were other maneuvers too: for example in Greece, leaving arms behind for the use of both competing guerrilla forces, anti-Communist (and pro-British) and Communist (pro-Russian) ones. In northern-most Norway a German evacuation in the winter of 1944–1945 was undertaken with the hope of clashes between advancing Russian and British commando forces in a vacuum. Before the German evacuation of Rome in June 1944 Hitler wanted Field Marshal Kesselring to engage with some kind of a negotiation with American generals about the open-city status of Rome. In view probably of Catholic but also of American opinion, he ordered his forces to leave Rome intact. Nor did he — contrary to widespread belief — order that Paris, left behind, ought to be destroyed or burned. He knew that throughout 1944 and 1945 Himmler was engaged in many kinds of tortuous and secret negotiations with Americans: Hitler seems to have tacitly consented to them; we know only one occasion (in February 1945) when he berated Himmler for such things. That same month he allowed his most rigid minion Ribbentrop to issue a directive to German diplomats (a "Sprachregelung") to try some contact with British and especially American diplomats, warning them of the dangers of Communism and of Russia's penetration into Europe. When in March 1945 the SS general Karl Wolff entered into actual negotiations with Americans about a partial capitulation of the German armies in Italy, Hitler not only was apprised of this but received Wolff in Berlin and, in his own way, wished him well in that endeavor.*

By that time Hitler no longer believed that he had power enough to drive a wedge between his enemies. When on the night of 12 April the news came of Roosevelt's sudden death, the excited Goebbels rushed over to him, brought champagne to the Führer's bunker, proclaiming that a turning point of the war

---

* See pages 172–173.

had come.* Hitler did no longer think that, though he still believed that a break among his enemies would come.

In one of his last "table conversations" he rued treatment of other subservient but not National Socialist governments during the war; in other words, that he had sustained certain "conservatives" rather than revolutionaries. Had he extended a welcome to the working masses, especially in Western Europe, National Socialism could have become the great wave of the then present and of the then future. There were reasons for him to think thus. Certainly in 1940, and for some time afterward, this seems to have been a possibility — among people who were, and not always because of pure opportunism, willing to accommodate themselves with what he and National Socialism then represented. This cut across classes. There were working-class districts in Paris where people looked at the Germans marching in with something like an amiable curiosity; there was Leopold III, king of the Belgians, who when visiting Hitler in November 1940 was deeply impressed: "Only once in a thousand years a man of his stature is born."†

"Only once." Thank we must God for this.

---

* He talked of the sudden death of the Tsarina Elizabeth, *the* turning point in the war against Frederick the Great, Elizabeth having been his determined enemy. (Goebbels also knew that Hitler had been reading Carlyle's admiring biography of Frederick.)

† Paul Belien, *A Throne in Brussels* (Charlottesville, Va., 2005), p. 213, citing H. De Man, *Le Dossier Leopold III* (Geneva, 1989), p. 33.

FIVE

The Germans' Two Wars, Heisenberg and Bohr

I begin with something that is (or should be) obvious. The history of the atomic bomb (more accurately: the history of the first three atomic bombs, Alamogordo, Hiroshima, Nagasaki) is part of the history of the Second World War. The history of these bombs — as indeed the history of every human product — is the history of the men and women who invented them, designed them, planned them, and constructed them. The history of science not only is inseparable from the history of scientists: it *is* the history of scientists. No scientists, no science. This is because history is not part of science, while "science" is part of the history of mankind.

The "causes" of the atom bomb are historical and, ultimately, personal; they are scientific and technical only on a secondary and mechanical level of "causes." The causes of the making of the bomb during the Second World War were Hitler, and also the persecution of Jews by his Germans. The first atomic bomb was made when it was made not merely because at a certain phase in the development of applied physics a certain stage of technical capacity was reached, but because at a certain time in history the fear had arisen in the minds of a few eminent scientists, most of them refugees in America, that German scientists might be building an atomic bomb for Hitler. Technically speaking, the important stages in the history of the atomic bomb were the splitting of a uranium nucleus by neutrons in Berlin in December 1938, the functioning of the first nuclear reactor in Chicago in December 1942, the exploding of the first bomb in New Mexico in July 1945, and the two bombs finally cast on Japan in August 1945. But the technical achievement of these stages must not obscure their main purposes, which, as in every historical event, were the results of personal choices, their sources having been the national, political, religious, intellectual, and ideological inclinations in the minds of responsible men.

At the very beginning of the war, more than two years before Pearl Harbor, the ruling powers of the United States were told that an atomic bomb could be made, and that it *must* be made, because Germany might be making it. The ruling powers of National Socialist Germany were told somewhat later that atomic bombs could be made but that the costs and the efforts and the duration of their production were unduly large. In both countries the construction of a nuclear reactor was necessary before the production of a nuclear bomb, but German scientists, though having come close, had not reached that stage before the end of the war and the total defeat of Germany. But my subject here is not the actual race between American and German bomb building — nor within that, the awful and unanswerable question of potentiality, of what could have happened had Hitler possessed atomic bombs.

◆ ◆ ◆

My subject includes a meeting between two scientists, the German Werner Heisenberg and the Danish Niels Bohr, in German-occupied Copenhagen in September 1941, about which many books and many dozens of articles and a very successful play have been written and international conferences assembled, more than sixty years after that event. Heisenberg and Bohr talked and listened to and understood and misunderstood each other. What Heisenberg said (or suggested) was (and remained) more significant than how Bohr responded to him. That imbalance (if that was what it was) was well nigh inevitable because of the very circumstances and conditions of their meeting and also what had preceded their conversations in September 1941.

Heisenberg and Bohr were among the greatest—and, perhaps, *the* greatest—physicists in the twentieth century. Surely they were the two leaders during the brief golden age of physics, 1924–1927, when Heisenberg's indeterminacy theory and Bohr's Copenhagen complementary interpretation superseded Einstein's still largely deterministic concept of physical reality. Heisenberg and Bohr were close allies at the time, defeating Einstein (who was unable and unwilling to accept the meaning of indeterminacy even against its evidences, and who tried in vain to disprove it during the last thirty years of his life). Heisenberg, fifteen years younger than Bohr, was his protégé. Soon Heisenberg's reputation rose ever higher. They regarded each other with mutual high esteem; but they were also close friends, talking about everything, spending skiing and mountain vacations together, enjoying music (Heisenberg was a good pianist).

Heisenberg went often to see Bohr in Copenhagen. Almost always they talked in German, but Heisenberg even learned to speak Danish more or less adequately. Heisenberg was German, Bohr was Danish and half-Jewish. This did not matter — surely not for some time.

In 1933 Hitler came to power in Germany. In the same year Heisenberg, at the age of thirty-two, won the Nobel Prize in physics. Like many patriotic Germans he saw something good in the end of the tottering Weimar Republic and in the national rejuvenation of which Hitler was the loudest drummer and most strident trumpeter. Heisenberg never became a National Socialist Party member. He regarded the excesses of Nazi rhetoric and behavior as regrettable — and, more important, as perhaps temporary: he thought and often said that things and people would settle down sooner or later, and then normal conditions of work and life could prevail. He helped to protect and to assist some Jewish physicists who were deprived of their jobs and felt compelled to leave Germany in 1933 and after. There were instances when he tried to persuade some of them not to leave or even to return (he so advised Max Born, a colleague whom he admired, in a letter, including a suggestion that not everything was bad — indeed, that there were some splendid things happening — in the new Germany). He refused to agree with two older German Nobel Prize–winning physicists, Philipp Lenard and Johannes Stark, who were furiously anti-Jewish, bellowing together against Einstein and his theories and "Jewish physics." Consequently in 1937 articles in a newspaper of the SS attacked Heisenberg (who was newly married then), calling him "a white Jew" on one occasion. Eventually, possibly because of the intervention of Heinrich Himmler (Heisenberg's mother knew Himmler's mother), Heisenberg was exonerated. His life and work could go on undisturbed; that same year he and Bohr met again, at an international physicists' conference.

In late 1938 something impossible occurred in a physics laboratory in Berlin, the meaning of which was immediately recognized by top physicists throughout the world. Otto Hahn (a decent and anti-Nazi German who was to receive the Nobel Prize for chemistry in 1945, while he was still interned in England) and Fritz Strassmann (an exceptionally principled Austrian whose bravery in helping and hiding Jews during the war would eventually be honored by the state of Israel) found, after repeated experiments, that uranium atoms could be split when bombarded by neutrons, that such a "fission" resulted in unexpected and powerful by-products. Hahn had visited Bohr in Copenhagen in October, speaking about his experiments in a lecture; Bohr was skeptical, but encouraged Hahn to go on with his experiments. A few weeks later, in December, Hahn's experiments concluded that fission could be achieved; that the split mass could be converted to energy. Heisenberg, teaching and working in Leipzig, learned of the Hahn achievement in Berlin from Carl Friedrich von Weizsaecker, who was, in a way, Heisenberg's protégé before that time.* Soon — in early 1939 — Hahn published the results of his experiments in a German scientific journal; a similar account would follow in a British one.

Less than a month after Hahn's conclusive experiment Bohr sailed for the United States, where he would spend part of a semester at Princeton. He understood the importance of the fission, but he thought that a consequent chain reaction could

---

*This young man with great powers of imagination and talent whom I, for one, have come to dislike because of his often arrogant and sinuous cleverness.

not lead to the making of a bomb, since the extent of such a construction would have to be so large as to be practically impossible. He said this in public, and kept to this belief for some time.* He sailed back to Copenhagen in April 1939, only a few weeks before Heisenberg arrived for an American lecture tour. He was invited to some of the same universities that Bohr had visited; and, more significantly, by many of the top physicists of the world now gathered in the United States, most of them refugees from Hitler's Germany and Mussolini's Italy. There is no evidence that Heisenberg behaved and talked with much compunction or caution or even excessive reserve with his colleagues, many of them Jewish, meeting them in their universities and sometimes in their homes. There are many records and memories of their conversations. They attempted to persuade him — so did eminent native-born American physicists — to remain in the United States, where he could work amid the best of conditions for his research, especially since the war in Europe was coming nearer and nearer. He would not give that a thought. His family and wife and first child were of course in Germany, awaiting his return. More important — certainly in the minds of his former colleagues and friends — was their concern with what Hitler's Germany represented and where the war could lead. One telling evidence of Heisenberg's convictions (and of his inclinations) is how he answered the great Italian physicist Fermi, an old friend (whose wife was Jewish). Talking with Fermi, he said that he felt

---

* Winston Churchill, not yet in the British government, was told of the importance of the Berlin discovery in the summer of 1939; but his advisers (especially Professor F. A. Lindemann, later to become Lord Cherwell) concluded, like Bohr, that the making of a bomb would be excessively costly and impractical. In retrospect, Churchill found this August 1939 memorandum important enough to include in the first volume of his Second World War history, *The Gathering Storm*, 1948, pp. 386–387.

a duty not to separate himself from young German scientists who, unlike himself, could not travel easily out of Germany. Fermi then got to the gist of the matter. The current German regime could force German physicists to work toward the potential manufacture of atomic weapons. Heisenberg said that he understood Fermi but that it was his opinion that such a technical achievement would in any event last longer than the war. In one, only one, instance Heisenberg spoke with something like anger. Fermi's wife said that anyone remaining in Germany must be mad; Heisenberg was hurt, and refuted her vehemently. He left New York in August 1939, sailing home on a half-empty German liner.

Heisenberg and Einstein had not met that summer in the United States. But exactly one month before the outbreak of the war, Albert Einstein signed a letter addressed directly to Franklin Roosevelt, advising him of the danger that the discovery of fission might enable Germany to construct a hitherto unimaginably powerful weapon, suggesting that the American government's support was needed for an American achievement of such a bomb. The idea of such a letter arose in the minds of the Hungarian-born physicists Leo Szilard and Eugene Wigner as early as June. Knowing of Einstein's reputation, Szilard and Wigner drove out to his summer dwelling to make him write to Roosevelt. Einstein wrote the letter and sent it to an acquaintance, a Jewish financier who had access to the president.* Let me repeat: my concern in this chapter is not the race between the American and the German bomb making. It is Heisenberg and

---

*The letter did not reach Roosevelt until October; it was a second letter given to Alexander Sachs, the abovementioned financier, signed by Einstein (again drafted by Szilard and Wigner) on 7 March 1940, that brought about the secret support by the American government, culminating in its results five years later.

Bohr: more precisely, how they regarded each other and how others saw them; even more precisely, how and why Heisenberg came to Bohr during the war, and how Bohr then came to regard Heisenberg's character and his politics. The sequence of events in 1939 suggests that many, if not most, of the refugee physicists, beyond and beneath their regret that they were not able to persuade Heisenberg to leave Germany for good, had begun to worry that Heisenberg would (or might) work for the achievement of nuclear explosives in Hitler's Third Reich. In sum: they trusted (and often admired) Heisenberg's science; they did not admire (and often did not trust) his politics. That, in essence, cast a shadow — at least in their minds — on his character.

"What kind of a man is Heisenberg?" the refugee scientists and their American colleagues asked themselves and one another. In a chapter on "The Question of Scientific Certitude"* a few years ago I wrote: "After all, everything that a man does depends on some kind of belief. He will speak and act in a certain way *because* he thinks that this kind of speaking or acting is better than another. 'What kind of a man' is not a simple question of category but one that inevitably depends on the inclinations of his mind and on the ideas he prefers to choose." And Heisenberg was, evidently, a German patriot, perhaps even a nationalist: his first duty was, perhaps to but certainly *in* Germany. That his former colleagues knew, and their own conclusions sprang therefrom.

On 1 September 1939 German armies invaded Poland and the Second World War began. Fourteen days later Heisenberg wrote a letter to Bohr, carried to Denmark by a mutual acquaintance, a Japanese physicist. "So once more I have the chance to write you. You know how sad I am about this entire development. But all of us have seen it coming, in America. I came back, since I belong

* *At the End of an Age,* p. 88.

here. You will surely understand this."* Bohr did not know that some of his American colleagues had begun to promote the prospect of constructing an atomic bomb; nor that the Heereswaffenamt (rough translation: Office of Military Weaponry) in Berlin had convened German physicists to discuss the problems and the prospect of manufacturing atomic explosives. He did not think that this was yet technically feasible (he said this in a lecture in Copenhagen later in 1939).

Suddenly, on 9 April 1940, Hitler ordered the German army and navy to occupy Denmark and Norway. Suddenly that brought about an additional drama in the lives of two physicists. Only a day before the German invasion Bohr had been in Oslo, at a scientific conference attended by the king of Norway himself; his ferry brought him back to Copenhagen on the very morning of the German invasion. The refugee scientist Lise Meitner, who had moved from Germany through Holland to Sweden in 1938, found herself in Copenhagen on 9 April, and then quickly fled back to her safe harbor in Sweden on the same day, taking with her among other things a letter from Bohr.

There is no evidence of any correspondence between Heisenberg and Bohr after April 1940. Surely Heisenberg was concerned with the fate of his former patron and friend; but it seems that he thought it best not to contact him until early September 1941.† That he respected Bohr was known by many people, including some within the government of the Third Reich; it may have contributed to the condition that Bohr's work in his Physics Institute in Copenhagen could continue undisturbed under the

* Helmut Rechenberg, "Kopenhagen 1941 und die Natur des deutschen Uranprojektes," manuscript, p. 7 (my translation). Rechenberg is the director of the Heisenberg-Institut (and Archive) in Munich.
† With one possible exception: see Weizsaecker's visit to Copenhagen in March 1941, page 120.

German occupation. But then that was part and parcel of the unique German treatment of Denmark. That country Hitler thought best to treat as something of a model protectorate. Normal civilian life in Denmark went on, with few restrictions, as also the life of the king. There were, as yet, no restrictions or discriminations forced on the lives of the — not numerous — Jews living in Denmark. Undoubtedly Bohr was observed occasionally by Germans, but he was able to work and to lecture; he even sent an article to a British scientific journal. He maintained some contact with American and British colleagues, partly through Sweden, partly through the remaining American legation in Denmark.

Of course he followed the news of the war with great anxiety and concern. But he had not heard directly from Heisenberg until September 1941 — a condition that must have been an element in his mind when his former friend and student appeared in Copenhagen, rather surprisingly, rather suddenly.

◆ ◆ ◆

Heisenberg arrived in Copenhagen early on 16 September, a Tuesday morning, having taken the night train with a sleeper from Berlin. He took a room in a tourist hotel. That very night he walked through the city to Bohr's house. That was the first of his three visits to Bohr and his wife. He left Copenhagen on Sunday the twenty-first.

The subject or focus of the new accumulated (and perhaps still growing) mass of books and papers and records of their meetings is the question (or riddle; or conundrum) of what happened between Heisenberg and Bohr in Copenhagen. Narrowing the focus further: What had Heisenberg said to Bohr? Or, even more accurately, what had Bohr heard him say? Heisenberg wrote in his published reminiscences (as did his wife in hers) about their meeting in general terms; Bohr, whose attention and, consequently, whose recollections were more acute than Heisenberg's, spoke about it to those close to him; and later, when a public controversy was about to emerge, wrote letters to Heisenberg, still extant, even though Bohr chose not to send them after all. In 2001 Bohr's descendants and the Bohr Archive in Copenhagen decided to make these drafts and letters public. These papers did not reveal much that was startlingly new. However, they confirmed Bohr's shock (a shock, more than a disappointment) with what Heisenberg had said to him in September 1941.

Now during those five days and evenings in Copenhagen, Heisenberg and Bohr met often, not only in Bohr's home but also among other physicists in Bohr's Institute; and then there was their now famous after-dinner walk, probably on Wednesday night the seventeenth. Their topics were the war, as it was or seemed at that time, and then, it seems only once, the prospect of the potential making of an atomic explosive. I believe—this being the purpose of this chapter—that these two themes were inseparable; indeed, that Bohr's bitter disappointments issued from Heisenberg's statements about the first even more than about the second.

◆ ◆ ◆

The controversy, or Bohr's possible understanding or misunderstanding of Heisenberg's intentions, was, and remains, inseparable from the actual conditions of Heisenberg's visit to Copenhagen. It seems that the very idea of his visit to Copenhagen came from C. F. von Weizsaecker. This is significant, and deserves some explanation. Weizsaecker was in Berlin and Heisenberg in Leipzig, but they had become close friends in the late 1930s and thereafter. And colleagues too: in the summer of 1940 Weizsaecker, on the spur of the moment, came up with a brilliant idea concerning nuclear particles. More important: his father, Ernst von Weizsaecker, state secretary in the German Foreign Ministry, was second only to Ribbentrop. He was of the older type of German diplomatist, not a convinced or even committed Nazi: Ribbentrop knew this but kept him on (so did Hitler, indeed to the very end: late in the war he appointed Weizsaecker to the post of German ambassador to the Holy See in Rome).* He wished Hitler were more prudent (he wrote a memorandum in April 1941 warning against a war in Russia); but he also wished that the Third Reich would win the war; surely he did not want Germany to lose it. In the 1920s he had been German minister to Denmark. It was through his recommendation and assistance that Heisenberg's journey to Copenhagen was arranged.

Academics and scholars will, or ought to, admit that often the main intention of meeting a particular friend or friends may be facilitated through the pretext of a conference, enabling them thus to meet. It seems that the original idea of Heisenberg's Copenhagen visit was Weizsaecker's. Weizsaecker had gone to Copenhagen already in March 1941, when he met Bohr. His and Heisenberg's main intentions were to meet Bohr and to talk to and with him. The occasion was to be an astrophysical conference in Copenhagen arranged by the German Scientific Institute, an institution established by the Third Reich. Two other German academics went to Copenhagen too. There were to be lectures, including one by Heisenberg, in that institute — where, except for the occasion of Heisenberg's lecture, many Danish

---

* He was tried in Nuremberg in 1948 and was thereafter acquitted. One of his sons, Richard von Weizsaecker, an honorable and intelligent man, was elected president of (West) Germany in 1984.

physicists declined to appear.* There were more get-togethers and lunches in Bohr's Institute. On one occasion Heisenberg spoke in Danish.

There is some evidence that before Heisenberg's arrival in Copenhagen, Bohr, and especially his wife, Margarethe, hesitated whether to invite Heisenberg to their house to dinner. They were uneasy with Heisenberg—in a way in which their Jewish colleagues in America had been suspicious of him in 1939, and probably also because of the silence from Heisenberg ever since the German occupation of Denmark;† even more probably, because they were unsure of what Heisenberg planned to do and how he would behave once in Copenhagen. But these hesitations soon dissipated. After all, Niels Bohr wanted to see Werner Heisenberg; Heisenberg contacted Bohr immediately after his arrival and well before the opening of the conference; on his first day he walked across the city late in the evening to get to the Bohrs'.

Neither of them had planned to discuss politics, which of course meant the war; but those intentions melted away fast. Already at the lunches and discussions in Bohr's Institute, Heisenberg talked about the war, in the presence of others. His—repeated—statements shocked and impressed Bohr. On at least two occasions Heisenberg said that Germany was winning the war—indeed, that Germany was close to winning it at that time. On other occasions, Heisenberg stiffly refuted statements by Bohr and others about the German treatment and behavior of occupied countries such as Poland.

---

*The dates of the conference (18–23 September) did not exactly coincide with Heisenberg's stay (16–21 September) in Copenhagen.
†Did Weizsaecker in March bring some kind of greeting or message from Heisenberg to Bohr in Copenhagen? Probably; but I have seen no evidence of that.

It is at least possible that Heisenberg's statements at these meetings — he knew that he could be observed by some people of the German secret services — were meant to protect himself in view of the powers in Berlin. But then his remarks about the war in the institute did not differ much from how he was talking privately in Bohr's home during and after their dinners. Moreover: yes, Bohr was permitted to live and work physically and professionally a largely free life in Hitler's model Danish protectorate; and to Heisenberg it seemed that, under the circumstances, this was perhaps enough. He could not or did not comprehend the depressing mental conditions of Bohr's life, of a half-Jewish scientist in German-occupied Denmark. Had he understood that better, he might have approached Bohr somewhat differently.

I shall yet return to Heisenberg's view of the war, but before that I must attempt to disentangle — necessarily imperfectly — the other, though related, matter between himself and Bohr: that of the prospect of atomic bombs. It is hardly questionable that a talk with Bohr about *that* topic was *the* main intention of Weizsaecker (and of Heisenberg) in arranging the trip to Copenhagen. Heisenberg brought up the problem or question of the prospect of atomic bombs only once, during their private walk and talk. That night Heisenberg spoke most of the time; Bohr, listening closely, was reticent. He was nervous and (understandably) suspicious. It seems that the talk, again, began with politics; that Heisenberg said that he believed Soviet Russia would soon be defeated, which was a good thing. He then said something about his and Weizsaecker's contacts with the German legation in Copenhagen, attempting to ensure that Bohr would be protected from interference with his person and his work; it seems that he proposed that it would be useful and desirable if Bohr would have some contact with the German legation. Then Heisenberg asked Bohr whether he understood, too, that now, after the successful fission experiments, atomic bombs could be made. This included a suggestion that this could (rather than would) be achieved in Germany and the war, if it lasted long enough, could be waged by atomic weapons. Then he seems to have made an even more oblique suggestion about how good it would be if perhaps physicists on both sides of the war (meaning the German war against the West) could refrain from working toward atomic weapons. Bohr's reactions to what Heisenberg was saying were bleakly negative. Heisenberg told that to Weizsaecker immediately after he returned to his hotel; he said that Bohr did not understand him and that their talk was a failure.

Bohr seems to have thought that Heisenberg brought up the suggestion that the making of a German nuclear bomb was a possibility with the intention of impressing him. Heisenberg seems to have thought that because of Bohr's potential and perhaps even actual contacts with physicists in Allied countries, some kind of a tacit agreement might be attempted to avoid making bombs. Bohr thought that such a secret agreement across the world was nonsense; in this Bohr was right. He also thought that Heisenberg may have been somehow attempting to frighten or even blackmail him with the suggestion that the making of an atomic bomb was after all possible in Germany too; in this Bohr was wrong.

The main documentary sources of this conversation are in the drafts of Bohr's letters to Heisenberg in 1957 that he then chose not to send. The origin of these unsent letters was Bohr's angry reaction to a book published in 1956, written by Robert Jungk (*Brighter Than a Thousand Suns*); Jungk proposed that while in America scientists were producing atomic bombs, in Germany Heisenberg and others had refused to do so. Ten years before that, in 1947, Heisenberg had visited Bohr in Copenhagen; they also met later, the last time in 1961 (Bohr died in 1962). Bohr was courteous to Heisenberg and later somewhat mellowed; but their prewar close friendship was not reborn.

There exists yet another document, recently found and made available by Heisenberg's family,* after the opening of the Bohr Archive. It is a long letter that Heisenberg wrote in Copenhagen on three evenings to his wife, mailed in Berlin after his return. Since it reveals much of Heisenberg's then views of his war as well as of how he saw Bohr, I must cite it in some detail.

He wrote the first portion of it probably on Wednesday the seventeenth (it may have been wrongly dated as the sixteenth, Tuesday, subsequently by his wife). It begins with an account of his train travel, and with his sentimental revisiting Copenhagen, with its churches and bells. "Late [last] night I walked under a clear and starry sky across the city, darkened, to Bohr. Bohr and his family are doing fine; he has aged a little. His sons are fully grown now. The conversation quickly turned to the human concerns and unhappy events of these times: about the human affairs the consensus is given; in questions of politics I find it difficult that even a man like Bohr can not separate out thinking, feeling, and hating entirely." Then something about Mrs. Bohr and children. "Later I was sitting for a long time with Bohr alone; it was after midnight when he accompanied me to the streetcar, together with Hans [Bohr]." He added another portion to the letter Thursday night. "Yesterday I was again with Bohr for the whole evening; aside from Mrs. Bohr and the children, there was a young English woman, taken in by the Bohrs, because she can not return to England.† It is somewhat weird to talk with an English woman these days. During the unavoidable political

---

*In Helmut Rechenberg, "Documentation and Reminiscences of the Bohr/Heisenberg Meeting in 1941," typescript; also in http://werner-heisenberg.unh.edu./copenhagen.htm.
†I think this was Miss Ray, the Bohr children's nanny.

conversations, where it naturally and automatically became my assigned part to defend our system, she retired, and I thought that was actually very nice of her." Next morning, with Weizsaecker, "we ate a meal on the Langelinie, all around us there were essentially only happy, cheerful people, at least it appeared that way to us. In general, people look so happy here. At night in the streets one sees all these radiantly happy young couples." "In Bohr's Institute we had some scientific discussions, the Copenhagen group, however, doesn't know much more than we do either. Tomorrow the talks in the German Scientific Institute are beginning, the first official talk is mine, tomorrow night. Sadly the members of Bohr's Institute will not attend for political reasons. It is amazing, given that the Danes are living totally unrestricted, and are living exceptionally well, how much hatred or fear has been galvanized here, so that even a rapprochement in the cultural arena . . . has become almost impossible . . . nobody wants to go to the German Scientific Institute on principle."* "Today I was once more, with Weizsaecker, at Bohr's. In many ways this was especially nice, the conversation revolved for a large part of the evening around purely human concerns. Bohr was reading aloud. I played a Mozart sonata (A-Major)." "On the way home the night sky was again star-studded."

Heisenberg made no mention of or even a suggestion about his nocturnal walk and talk with Bohr, and nothing about the subject of nuclear prospects in this letter to his wife, mailed in Berlin; nothing, either, in his report to the German Ministry of Education that he wrote immediately after his return to Leipzig. Yet the main intention of both Weizsaecker and Bohr in

---

* That noon at a reception and lunch at the German legation, Heisenberg was pleased that the American minister, a lady, was there and talked animatedly with her German host. The letter continues on Saturday night.

arranging this Copenhagen journey, including the conference, was to establish contact and perhaps some kind of arrangement with Bohr. That intention was primarily political. They could not expect much technical information or scientific advice from Bohr, who — as we have seen — had been more skeptical about the prospect of an eventual construction of atomic weapons than Heisenberg and others; and who was both older and less energetic than Heisenberg and other younger physicists. They knew, too, that, even under the German occupation of Denmark, Bohr had possibilities of contact with other colleagues on the other side of the war, not only in or through Sweden but even to England and the United States.

◆ ◆ ◆

That atomic bombs could be made, and that eventually they could change the course and the result of the war, was knowledge current among the leaders of the Third Reich, including Hitler, Goebbels, and some of their top generals. That, at a very important conference in June 1942, Heisenberg said to Hitler's top armament minister Speer that an atomic bomb could be made but that its construction would take a long time and require immense efforts and expenditures is now well known. According to some people this proves that Heisenberg took a stand against making a bomb for Hitler; according to others Heisenberg's continuing work on building a nuclear reactor proves simply that he and his Germans were unable to build one. Both arguments are exaggerations. It was not until the last months of the war that Americans learned that Heisenberg and the Germans were not building a bomb. And: why? "Intentions," as Samuel Johnson said, "must be gathered from acts." True — even though (as also in the nature of subatomic particles) actuality is hardly separable from potentiality. During the war, many refugee physicists in

America thought that Heisenberg was both able and willing to support the building of a German atomic bomb. The Austrian and originally Jewish Lise Meitner, a very good scientist, who knew Heisenberg well before she fled Germany in 1938,* wrote in 1945 that "the way [Heisenberg] turned up in Denmark in 1941 is unforgettable."† Einstein, in a remark written well after the war, said that Heisenberg was "a big Nazi."‡ That was nonsense and, perhaps worse than nonsense: untrue.

Closer to the truth, there was a duality in Heisenberg's mind, a duality that existed and still exists in the minds of many of his countrymen. He did not want Germany to lose the war. At the same time he regretted the war — the war against the West, that was.§ One important, though indirect, evidence of this is the message that Heisenberg's colleague Fritz Houtermans chose to give, bravely, to Fritz Reiche, an engaging and modest Jewish physicist who as late as March 1941 had received a visa and an exit permit to the United States. "Please remember [there] to tell the interested people the following thing. We are trying here hard, including Heisenberg, to hinder the idea of making a bomb. But the pressure from above . . . Please say all this: that Heisenberg will not be able to withstand longer the pressure

---

* She was already a refugee in Stockholm when Heisenberg wrote her on the occasion of her sixtieth birthday, "[You have] enriched our science and thereby our entire lives," thanking her "for having this work in Germany, and for all you have done for German physics." This emphasis on Germany disappointed Meitner. Ruth Lewin Sime, *Lise Meitner: A Life in Physics* (Berkeley, 1996), pp. 225–226.

† She meant "unforgivable." Sime, *Lise Meitner,* p. 310.

‡ Quoted in the *New York Times,* 24 April 2004.

§ Another duality: he did not wish Germany to lose; yet once or twice during the war he wrote or talked about an international (more precisely: supranational) community of scientists' moral concern about the applications of science for the sake of mankind.

from the government to go very earnestly and seriously into the making of the bomb."* Note, however, that this happened before Heisenberg's visit to Copenhagen, and before the German war against Russia.

There are more than dualities, there are many motives as well as purposes within human intentions and actions. We cannot exactly know — and perhaps neither Heisenberg nor Bohr could exactly know — what was the exact purpose of Heisenberg's mention of the potentiality of a German bomb to Bohr. But we may be fairly sure that at least one of them included his knowledge of Bohr's — actual as well as potential — contacts with Allied physicists through Sweden or otherwise,† contacts that somehow continued until Bohr's flight from Denmark in 1943.

Ambiguity and ambivalence: they may overlap but they are not the same. It may be argued that Heisenberg's inclinations involving a German-made bomb were ambiguous. Had he been told: "No matter how long and expensive the effort. Go ahead" — would he have declined or sabotaged the plan? Probably not; but at the same time it is also probable that Speer's response, effectively not to go ahead, gave him a sense of relief. In any event, he went on working on the making of a nuclear reactor. He said, several times during the war, even close to its end, that he did not wish that Germany would lose it; he did not want Germany to be defeated, though he did not wish the National Socialist Third Reich to be victorious. But then, sadly until the very end, Germany and the National Socialist Third Reich were not separable — except in his mind and in the minds of many million other Germans.

*Thomas Powers, *Heisenberg's War* (New York, 1993), pp. 106–107, recounting Reiche's recollections in 1961.
†They include Bohr's visit from German-occupied Denmark to neutral Stockholm in the spring of 1941.

That was ambiguity, rather than ambivalence. His mind (and, again, that of many million other Germans) was marked, rather, by an ambivalence. He regretted Germany's war against the West, but supported the German war against Russia, the Soviet Union. There are evidences of his regret of the first: among them his respect for the young Englishwoman in Bohr's house in Copenhagen (in his letter to his wife) and, in a letter to his mother in November 1940 about Chamberlain's death. "There [in England] verily a nation keeps fighting and one must really admire how much people in London are able to bear."* These were not the words — and sentiments — of a "Nazi."

Again — as in the minds of many other Germans — his ambivalence was part and parcel of his anti-Communism. A sharp memory of his early youth was the brief "Soviet" episode in Munich in 1919. He voiced his contempt for and fear and hatred of Communism often; in August 1939 his reaction to the first rumors of a German pact with the Soviet Union was one of incredulity. And now we come to September 1941 and his statements in Copenhagen,† at the time when the German armies were racing ahead in Russia, encircling Leningrad, ready to break into Kiev, closer and closer every day to Moscow; when the Soviet Union (as Stalin himself admitted to Churchill in early September) "was on the verge of collapse." As late as 1944 he would say: "Must we hope that we lose the war?" The year before, visiting Holland,

---

*Letter of 11 November 1940 in *Liebe Eltern! Briefe aus kritischer Zeit 1918 bis 1945,* ed. by his daughter Anna Maria Hirsch-Heisenberg (Munich, 2003), p. 313. "What do you think now that Chamberlain has died? I cannot but think with sympathy of a man who truly wanted peace but whose politics ended in a total shipwreck. . . . The English have it very tough now, but the death of one man means little in politics."
†Alas, this went together with Heisenberg's dismissal of other Eastern European nations, as he said on one occasion, "who are not able to govern themselves."

he told a Dutch physicist that it has "always been the mission of Germany to defend the West and its culture against the onslaught of eastern hordes . . . and so, perhaps, a Europe under Germany leadership might be the lesser evil."*

◆ ◆ ◆

Heisenberg's wishes and his purposes in Copenhagen were not wholly different from those of Rudolf Hess, who a few months before had taken upon himself the task of flying to Britain, to attempt to persuade the British to make peace or at least an armistice with Germany. In their different ways both Hess and Heisenberg regretted the war between Germany and Britain (with America coming closer and closer to the British side). Both thought that Germany was winning: Hess shortly before the German invasion of Russia, Heisenberg (with even more reason) after that. Both of them thought in terms of the Two-War Idea.

What was — and still is — the German Two-War Idea? It is that Germany fought two wars: one against the Western democracies, the Anglo-American side, the other against Russia, the incarnation of Communism; that one was regrettable and avoidable, while the other was not; and that regrettable, too, was the fact that Germany's Anglo-American opponents did not understand this. Appearances and attractions of the Two-War Idea persist even now. They were at the bottom of the *Historikerstreit*, the historians' controversy of 1986; and they are stated and promoted by certain Germans (and also be some British "revisionists") to this day.

There is plenty of evidence that the Two-War Idea accorded with German sentiments as well as with German political cal-

---

* Quoted in Sime, *Lise Meitner,* p. 303. See also the last paragraph of this chapter.

culations in 1941. It was there in the dreadful difference in the treatment of Western and Russian prisoners of war: one million of the latter were starved to death in German prison compounds in 1941. It was there among respectable non-Nazis such as Heisenberg, the most telling example being that of Archbishop (later Cardinal) Clemens August von Galen, who, from his pulpit in Munster in August 1941, attacked the Nazi practice of euthanasia and who, in the same sermon, praised the invasion of Russia as a crusade against atheistic Communism. (Hitler chose to leave Galen alone). Such a duality, or ambivalence, was there in Heisenberg's mind, too. At the same time, what he and Weizsaecker were trying to in Copenhagen was something more intricate than the duality of that archbishop and than the intention of Hess. After all, Heisenberg was attempting to contact not a British duke but an old friend, a Danish physicist; and there was both naïveté and idealism in his attempt to suggest something to Allied physicists by way of Bohr. At the same time his attempt was not at all devoid of political considerations and calculations.

After all, the German government supported Heisenberg's mission. However, *German government* is an imprecise term. The government of the Third Reich was both autocratic and polycratic. Some of its organs, some of its people had different inclinations. There was the Abwehr; there was the Gestapo; there was the foreign minister and men such as Weizsaecker's father; there was the SS; there were Canaris, Ribbentrop, Himmler, different men. Different, yes: but the Two-War Idea, in some ways, was shared by all of them, and by the German people at large. And a consequence of the Two-War Idea was that of multiple German attempts — including not a few approved by Hitler — to split the, to them, unnatural coalition of British and Americans and Russians.

The German regime (or at last some members of it) knew of Bohr's contacts abroad; that Bohr corresponded with Allied scientists through Sweden (including a principal British physicist, Sir James Chadwick). I am not saying that they had access to that kind of clandestine correspondence. (In one instance they did.) But they, for political reasons, allowed a relative measure of private freedoms in Denmark, where Bohr, too, went on living and working, though under dark clouds and surveillance, until he fled to Sweden and therefrom to Britain in 1943. I am not saying that they facilitated Bohr's escape to the Allies. I am saying that in 1941 they thought it to be in their interest to permit the existence of certain indirect contacts with the Western Allies, since they saw at least potential advantages in such. That was their, more than occasional, practice throughout the rest of the war.

Heisenberg's purposes and his failure to come close to a meeting of minds with Bohr in Copenhagen were complicated. The "uncertainties" of what happened then were historical, personal, national, and political — as were the "causes" of the atomic bomb.

◆ ◆ ◆

Had only Germans and British not fought each other (in 1940 or 1941 or thereafter): this was the wish (and often the daydream) of many "conservatives," not only in Germany but throughout Europe, for many of them till this day. That would have allowed the Germans to clean up Russia and Communism; and so what? At the bottom of this wish (but not very deep down) was and is the belief that Communism and Russia were more dangerous (and more evil) than were National Socialism and Germany. That is a half-truth. But half-truths are more dangerous — and enduring — than are lies.

SIX

Rainbow Five

Rainbow Five was the code name of the American strategic war plan, according to which in the event of a two-ocean and two-front war, administering the defeat of Germany (together with America's allies) must occur first and foremost, before defeating Japan. The plan was adopted in 1941, months before Pearl Harbor, and before the German invasion of Soviet Russia. The latter, in retrospect, was the most consequential event of the Second World War. But Rainbow Five — secret as it was, unannounced to a then still divided American people — was hardly less consequential. How it came about is the subject of this chapter.

But before discussing its conception and its birth there must be some contemplation of its consequences. After all, we can essay the relative importance of events only from their consequences. So — where were the consequences of Rainbow Five for the greatest of world wars and perhaps for the history of an entire century?

In 1940 and 1941 the Germans almost won the Second World War. Even after that they could have forced out something like a partial victory, with one or the other of their great adversaries compelled to cease fighting against them. In 1940 the British held out against the Germans; but they were not capable of winning a war against them. They were worse off than they had been against Napoleon when they would and could win with the help of powerful continental allies. In 1941 and thereafter they could not win, not even with Russia as their ally. With Russia, probably not; with Russia and America, almost certainly yes. *With America:* that was decisive for Russia too. Russia and Britain together could — perhaps — hold the Germans, but not drive them back to Berlin, not force them to surrender. For that the United States was needed, with its armies, to land in Europe, and with its gigantic industry of war. The British held up the Germans in 1941 and the Russians held them in 1941 and 1942. Not many American supplies reached them at that time. After that the American contribution became a flood. The tide of the American flood of materials reached Russia in 1944 and 1945, when it may no longer have been sorely needed, but that is another story. But behind that lies another untold, and often unthought, story: that Britain and America together, with all of their maritime supremacy, may not have been able to wrestle Germany down, without Russia as their ally on land. That was not what Franklin Roosevelt thought in 1941; neither did the army and navy staff planners who constructed Rainbow Five earlier in that year. Should they be criticized for that? No: Rainbow Five is to their credit.

◆ ◆ ◆

"The war to end wars," "to make the world safe for democracy": these were President Woodrow Wilson's ideas and slogans at the end of the First World War. They accorded neither with reality nor with the subsequent political choices of the American people, with the Republicans, with their large popular majorities in 1918 and 1920 and thereafter. Most Republicans were anti-internationalist. They were, by and large, the American *nationalist* party, with few exceptions, from their very beginning until the present day.* Republican presidents, such as Harding and Coolidge, spoke of the return from war to American "normalcy"; but they did not wish even to consider independence for the Philippines or for Cuba; they favored and often promoted American naval and military interventions in the Caribbean; they also kept funding and building up the United States Navy, which, notwithstanding the naval disarmament agreements reached at the Washington Conference in 1922, remained the prime navy in the world throughout the twenty years between the world wars — during which the United States Army dwindled to fewer than 140,000 officers and men, not more than the seventeenth-largest in the world.

Much of this was involved with a kind of American split-mindedness, rejecting American involvements in Europe while insisting not only on American interests but on an American presence in the western Pacific and on occasion even in China. But beyond and beneath such inclinations about America's destiny being ever westward (and the age-old American illusions about China) there existed a powerful element of political and strategic reason and common sense. The United States (and especially the United States Navy) ought to be prepared for an eventual armed conflict with Japan, probably in the western Pacific.

---

* A condition obscured by the shortsightedness of political commentators and of most historians, unaware of the difference between nationalism and patriotism, and between a nationalist and an — old-fashioned — patriot.

Before — and for some years even after — Japan's stunning victory in the Russian-Japanese War of 1904–1905, both American public opinion and government regarded the rise of Japanese power and presetige in the Far East with some benevolence.* But during and after the First World War, Japan's imperial expansion in the western Pacific and in China and, for a time, in the Russian Far East began to concern Americans, particularly some people in Washington, and the American naval leadership. In 1914, employing the pretext of joining the war against the German empire, the Japanese occupied two German-governed ports on the China coast, and — strategically and geographically more important — they took over a group of former German possessions, a scatteration of islands in the western Pacific (the Carolinas, Marianas, and Marshall Islands). Since 1902 Britain had had an alliance with Japan. In February 1917 the British Admiralty asked for Japanese destroyers to join the Allied fleet in the Mediterranean, in exchange for Britain's acceptance of these newly acquired Japanese possessions in the Pacific, thousands of miles from Malaysia, Australia, and the Philippines. In 1920 Japan took advantage of the Russian civil war. Japanese troops appeared in Vladivostok and attempted to penetrate further into the Russian Far Eastern provinces, from which they then withdrew, mostly because of American pressure. Next year the British chose not to renew their twenty-year-old alliance with Japan. Aware of American concern with Japan, the British would do nothing to endanger their good relations with the United States. In 1922, during the Washington Conference, the United States and Britain stood side by side, arriving at a naval armament ratio

---

*There was a crisis in 1907 when California passed discriminatory and restrictive legislation against people of Japanese origin. This was then smoothed over by a "gentlemen's agreement" between Washington and Tokyo.

of 5 and 5 (United States and Britain) and 3 (Japan) in the tonnage of battleships, and reaching also a general (though imprecise) agreement to avoid any further partition of China (this again mostly with Japanese ambitions in mind).

More important, for our purposes, than a survey of American-Japanese political relations is the actual strategy and war planning of the United States Navy developing continually in the 1920s and 1930s, with the code name Orange, considering a potential war with Japan — until in 1940–1941 the Orange designation and its plans changed to Rainbow.

The American Navy's War College was established before the Army War College. Before we consider their collaboration and adoption of the Rainbow versions in 1940–1941, we must contemplate the wide general scene, more consequential than the different and necessarily speculative war games limned by selected officers of both services in their colleges. The tendency to prefer and fund the navy rather than the army was constant during at least half a century before 1941. This had less to do with American traditions than with the unique geographical situation of the United States, between the two largest oceans of the world. Added to this was the then broadly accepted conviction that sea power, even more than land power, ruled the world. *The Influence of Sea Power on History* was the title of a famous work by the American Admiral Alfred Thayer Mahan (1890). It is an odd coincidence that the old Mahan not only influenced but wrote to the then young Franklin Roosevelt, who was assistant secretary of the navy in 1914, warning the latter against an official American acquiescence to the Japanese acquisition of the Micronesian islands. Roosevelt was a constant believer in the primacy of sea power. As late as in 1941 he wrote to Churchill that sea power was the key to history and to victory. That was no longer so, as Hitler, among others, saw it: internal combustion motors made it possible for armies to move faster on land than on sea, among other things, depriving the British of strategic advantages they had had for three centuries at least.

But that is another story. What belongs here is that American public opinion, as well as popular sentiment, as well as the navy, considered war against Japan as the — relatively — most likely possibility of an American war in the future: a war in the Pacific, not in the Atlantic; a war that would probably be framed as a contest between two great navies. (The Japanese broke their naval limitations in 1934 and were building a larger and larger navy, including the then largest battleship of the world.) These American war plans did not call for an eventual invasion of Japan, and often not even for a primacy of the American defense of the Philippines, which were too far from the American naval bases in Hawaii, Guam, Wake, and Midway — in the eastern half of the vast Pacific Ocean. Men such as General Douglas MacArthur who were sanguine about the security of American bases in the Philippines were wrong.* The different plans of the commanders and of what could be called the general staff of the navy moved back and forth from a concept of securing the American governance of the eastern half of the Pacific with other plans of thrusting, mostly through Micronesia, into the western Pacific, including a support of the Philippines. These strategic speculations did

---

* Major, later General Lawton Collins of the Army War College in 1939: "We cannot, even as conditions are today, reinforce the Philippines. We are going to lose them right away. We are 9,000 miles away; the Japanese next door." This is the place to name the three most important studies on American war plans, leading to Rainbow Five: Henry G. Gole, *The Road to Rainbow: Army Planning for Global War, 1934–1940* (Annapolis, Md., 2002), whence the quotation of Collins, p. 97; *U.S. War Plans, 1938–1945,* ed. Steven T. Ross (Boulder, Colo., 2002); Edward S. Miller, *War Plan Orange: The U.S. Strategy to Defeat Japan, 1897–1945* (Annapolis, Md., 1991), by an admirable amateur historian.

not much concern the American people and their public representatives — surely not until 1940–1941. Before that, for most Americans involvements across the Pacific were more easily accepted — or, perhaps more precisely: less repulsive and less feared — than American involvements across the Atlantic, in Europe. To most: but not to all; and it is therefore to these divisions in American opinions and sentiments I must now turn.

◆ ◆ ◆

Admiral Mahan may have been wrong (though only in the long run, and beyond his lifetime) about the primacy of sea power in history; but he was not wrong about the primacy of public opinion in the history of American democracy. A few years before his death he wrote: "The prime uncertainty was whether the American public would tolerate a lengthy war, say of a year or two years' duration, for goals not vital to national survival." He was "certain that it could not."*

Mahan was thinking at that time about a naval war between the United States and Japan. He did not live to see his country's participation in the First World War in 1917. And: how could anyone in 1917 foresee the coming of a Second World War twenty years later?

Nineteen-seventeen was, of course, a great reversal after three hundred years during which people and armies moved across the Atlantic westward. Now, for the first time, more than one million Americans were sent across eastward, to help decide a great European war. They were supported by the American people, with an unbridled kind of enthusiasm, at least for awhile. Yet there was a division among the people of the United States in 1917, as about any and every war or prospect of war in their

* Miller, *War Plan Orange,* p. 29.

history since 1794 (or indeed even in 1776). In 1917 that division was largely one-sided: only six senators and fifty congressmen voted against Wilson's declaration of war on Germany, a division that seems to have represented rather accurately the division of American opinions and sentiments at that time (which is not always the case with the count of congressional votes). Twenty years later there was another, more inchoate, roiling and confusing and confused but also deep and consequential division of American popular sentiment and public opinion about a potential war, again involving the United States with Europe. That was the division usually defined as that between Isolationists and Interventionists, rising to the fore in 1937 and existing during the four eventful years thereafter.

"Isolationists" vs. "Interventionists": these designations are not entirely wrong, but they are also imprecise. *Isolationism* became a widely accepted and employed term in the language only in the 1920s; American "exceptionalism" and American "nationalism" apply to much of the same phenomenon: the United States had and has maintained and must maintain its own national interests; it must not involve itself in the conflicts of Europe; it must not invest American wealth and, worse, blood in wars of Europe; indeed, America must not move in the direction of Europe.* But American "isolationism" was not simple. It stood against American involvement in Europe rather than against American involvement in Asia. Isolationists as well as Interventionists believed that the United States was the best and freest country in the world, "the last best hope of mankind," as Lincoln had said. Both Isolationists and Interventionists also

---

* Hence also the restrictive Immigration Acts of 1921 and 1924: there must be fewer and fewer immigrants from Europe, especially from southern and eastern Europe, crowds of people admitted to the United States to become citizens of the Republic.

believed—in their different ways—that what was good for America was good for the world. There were isolationists among Republicans as well as among Democrats; among American imperialists and American pacifists; among American traditionalists as well as among American radicals; among Americans of German origin but also among Americans of Irish or Scandinavian or Scottish origin; among American Catholics as well as among American Protestants and Jews; among American populists and among American progressives. The important matter, for our purposes here, is that these sentiments reached their peak around 1937—when National Socialist Germany and Fascist Italy and Imperial Japan were rising and expanding their reach.

This was the result of the slowness of the momentum of the tides of public opinion that Tocqueville had foreseen. The first reactions against America's entry into the First World War in 1917, and particularly against the propaganda of the uniquely German guilt for the war, appeared among a minority of American radicals and liberals, of academics and intellectuals after 1920; but it took often more than a dozen years of such opinions to infiltrate the wider public and its representative congressmen and senators. In 1937 the so-called Ludlow Amendment, requiring that any American declaration of war must be preceded by and dependent on a national popular referendum, had dozens of supporters in Congress, though it did not come about;* yet in the same year both houses of Congress passed a Neutrality Act with large majorities. In October 1937 President Roosevelt made a significant speech in Chicago, proposing a "quarantine" against aggressor states of the world—an entirely impractical idea but,

---

* As late as in February 1939 a Gallup Poll reported that 58 percent of Americans agreed that "in order to declare war Congress should be required to obtain the approval of the people by means of a national vote."

still, suggesting a turn away from isolationism. The press reaction against this Quarantine Speech, while far from uniform, made Roosevelt retreat — at least for a while.*

On 5 November 1937, one month to the day of Roosevelt's Quarantine Speech, Hitler convened his top generals and ordered them to prepare for a European war, if must. If must: this was not yet a definite plan; he mentioned Austria, Czechoslovakia; he made almost no mention of Britain or of Soviet Russia, at the edges of Europe; he hoped that Britain might yet acquiesce in a German domination of Central and of most of Eastern Europe, with France willy-nilly following the British lead. He made no mention of the United States. Neither he, nor his generals or admirals, were thinking about a world war. There was another, to him eventually fatal, element in his mind. He thought that he would not live long, that time was working against him — and against Germany, whose potential enemies would be gaining strength during the coming years. This was not necessarily true: but his thinking made it so. That led to his speeding up his timetable in 1938 and 1939. Thereafter it led to his nearly incredible German triumphs in 1940 and 1941 and 1942 — and, thereafter, to his and Germany's catastrophe and collapse. But we are running ahead of our story, whose focus is the United States and, at its top, Franklin Delano Roosevelt.

* The Roosevelt administration was by no means "interventionist" from the beginning. It was anti-imperialist and antinationalist in the sense that it reduced American military interventions in the Caribbean, it recognized the Soviet Union, it improved relations with Mexico, it promised independence for the Philippines and abolished the American military protectorate over Cuba. (Alger Hiss began his political career in 1934 as counsel of the extreme-isolationist Nye Committee investigating American interventionists' profits [those of munitions makers, for example] of 1917. Ten years later the Communist-connected Hiss had risen high in the ranks of American internationalists.)

He recognized the meaning of Hitler. Perhaps in the sense of Pascal's profound maxim, Roosevelt understood more than he knew. At the same time he both knew and understood the width and the depth of American popular feeling against war, against involvement in Europe. In that same month of November 1937 there was a sudden episode, a crisis with Japan, whose fliers attacked and sank an American gunboat in a Chinese port, by accident or otherwise. The Japanese government apologized and paid reparations for the damages; but many Americans were already disturbed by the sight of Japan's aggressive march into China. Hitler's reputation in America was getting worse and worse. Yet for most Americans another war with Germany was still unthinkable, while for many of them the prospect of a naval and air war with Japan probably less so.

But now came three years, so momentous and dramatic and incredible in retrospect that seventy years and three generations later even their brief summary is a challenge to a historian's craft. First Germany rose to tower over most of Europe; then Hitler started a war; in less than a year he conquered most of what was still left of Europe; France was trampled down in a few weeks; only Britain and Soviet Russia, on the edges of the continent, were not yet under Hitler's sway; Italy and Japan had become his allies. The people of the United States were made increasingly uneasy by the sights and sounds of all of this. Few of them had any understanding or sympathy for Germany's cause; but they were still divided and their minds were split. Yes, Americans must help people who were standing against Germany, but America must not enter that war. The propositions of this division changed from month to month; but the different categories of their minds were often inchoate. Their president's mind was not. The concerns of his mind were different: he was determined to see Hitler crushed and to help bring that about; but at the same time he knew, and perhaps even overestimated, the American people's reluctance to enter a second world war. He was reluctant to march them into war; and he was unwilling to tell them openly what he really thought. He took one step after another to thwart Hitler: secret moves, half-open moves, other more open steps, still short of war. Their list may be too long to detail here. He hoped — in vain — that Hitler would attack American ships or forces somewhere in the Atlantic, brutally and conspicuously enough to free his, Roosevelt's hands, making it possible for him to propose a declaration of war. That Hitler would not do. He knew what Roosevelt wanted.

Roosevelt knew Europe (and the Far East) better than his presidential predecessors, particularly Wilson. By late 1938 he was encouraging and confidentially supporting foreign statesmen and politicians who opposed Germany and Japan. They included Churchill even before Churchill became the prime minister of Britain. But then, immediately then, came the crunch. Suddenly, within a few days in May 1940 it seemed that France was crumbling; and so might Great Britain. Roosevelt thought that then, if worse came to worst, the great British fleet would come over to the western Atlantic shores, to join the American (and Canadian) navies. No, said Churchill (whose relationship with Roosevelt was not yet what it would become later). He was not a man who would surrender to Hitler, no matter what; but if Britain were invaded and trampled down, her fleet would be the only asset that a new peace-making government would possess for the sake of getting some consideration from a triumphant Germany. As the year 1940 went on that awful prospect faded. Roosevelt now made move after move to assist Britain, at first with a few old destroyers; then with a declaration of Lend-Lease, making America the Arsenal of Democracy; then sending the United States Navy forward into the center of the Atlantic, occupying British naval bases and then Greenland and Iceland. How and when Roosevelt would arrive at an open war with Germany was still unkown and uncertain. But of one matter he was certain: even in the case of an American war with Japan, the priority and the primacy must be the defeat of Germany.

So far as building up of the American armed forces went there was not much secrecy (and there was no need for that): most isolationists were not pacifists, and the American people, as almost always, supported a massive strengthening of their armed forces. As early as in November 1939 the president summoned his main military and naval advisers to the White House, to proposed a giant aircraft construction program together with the rebuilding of the army and of the army air force. Within sixteen months the size of the army grew almost tenfold: from 140,000 men to 1.25 million. In May 1940 Roosevelt ordered fleet movements in the eastern Pacific at a time when Japan seemed to be tempted to occupy British and French and Dutch colonies in the Far East;* but by early 1941 he was against any further large buildup of the navy in the Pacific. Most capital ships were allotted to the Atlantic. The "decisive theater" was Europe. "The predominant enemy" was Germany.†

Fortunately for the nation, and fortunately for the world, this was not Roosevelt's view alone. Rainbow Five was not his draft — though in accord with his inclinations so it was.

◆ ◆ ◆

The Naval War College was established in 1884, the Army War College in 1901. They were, by and large, American adaptations of the high military and navy institutes of the great European

---

* See Miller, *War Plan Orange*, p. 510.
† Miller, *War Plan Orange*, p. 314.

Powers and of Britain; but both their compositions and their functions were also different. They were less intertwined with the government than were those institutes in most other countries; in turn, the American government paid less attention to them than were the customs elsewhere. Still they were training institutes on a high level, with officers selected from the more promising graduates of Annapolis and West Point. Most of them would eventually reach the rank of admiral and general. The Naval War College classes were seldom larger than seventy-five, surely not before 1941.

Their functions included planning for wars. This should not be misunderstood. War games and the planning of wars have been a standard exercise and task of such establishments throughout the world. Theoretical as such plans necessarily were (and are), they were mental exercises, though with consequences to their governments, influential in setting the course of ships of state. But in the American tradition and practice of government there was and could be nothing like a Schlieffen Plan.* The Senate and the House in Washington were generally uninformed of the colleages' war plans. This customary lack of interest even included such senators and congressmen who were chairmen and members of committees dealing with military affairs.† In that dangerous June of 1940, in the very days when France was collapsing (and when the Republican Party could have nominated an isolationist candidate for the approaching presidential election), there

---

* The plan (1905) of the German General Staff, designing the entire strategy of the German state and its armies for the next European war, with fateful consequences in 1914.
† "The State Department kept a wary distance from the idea of war." "The secretaries of war and the navy and their assistant secretaries rarely injected themselves into the planning work of their uninformed subordinates." Miller, *War Plan Orange*, pp. 11, 12.

was a sudden change. President Roosevelt reconstructed his cabinet, moving toward what may be called a national government. He dismissed his secretaries of war and the navy, Harry Woodring and Charles Edison, both of them more or less isolationists (Woodring more than Edison), replacing them with Henry Stimson and Frank Knox, men with more experience, Republicans but not isolationists, willing to commit themselves to an involvement of the United States on the side of Britain. Cabinet government is not how the American ship of state is directed or ruled, but after 1940 there existed something like Roosevelt's war cabinet. Perhaps equally important was the newly established position of Admiral William D. Leahy as the president's chief of staff, appointed to the White House after having been chief of naval operations from 1937 to 1939.

The Naval War College was seventeen years older than the Army War College, and for a long time its importance and influence was the greater of the two. The reasons for that are obvious. The navy was the prime defensive arm of the United States; its presence was indispensable in the two greatest oceans of the world; it had to be the principal power at least in one half of them, in the western Atlantic and in the eastern half of the Pacific.* And then, at least as important as this American naval tradition was the recognition, soon after 1920, that the most (and perhaps the only) likely American war in the future would be one with Japan.

"Orange" was the code name of the plan of a war against

---

* Miller, *War Plan Orange*, p. 16, about "the shared values of Newport and Washington. They believed in America's destiny as a great power and the rightness of its imperial span," including bases overseas. "They regarded the Royal Navy as a role model, especially admiring its offensive temperament. They agreed that the proper goal of a great power at war should be total victory."

Japan. ("Black" with Germany, "Red" with Britain — as late as in the 1920s.) During the 1920s and early 1930s the planners of the Naval War College calculated the requirements and the plotting of such a war in the Pacific. "War Plan Orange, the secret program of the United States to defeat Japan, was in my opinion history's most successful war plan," Miller wrote.* Yet, with my very great respect due to this excellent historian, I must amend (rather than dismiss) his phrase of "history's most successful war plan." By 1940 there was a new world situation that the planners — certainly not before, say, 1935 — could not foresee. This was the prospect of two world wars, simultaneously, one against Germany, the other against Japan, with Germany ruling almost all of Europe and coming close to winning the war against Britain. We now know how reasonably, nay, admirably, the planners of the navy faced this prospect, in large accord with the army and with the president, acquiescing in the replacement of "Orange" with the newer "Rainbow," directing their primary attention to the Atlantic even more than to the Pacific, with which the Orange planners had wrestled and now had to let stay, though only temporarily, unresolved: the very nature of a war with Japan.

Should the American navy thrust into the western Pacific soon after the start of such a war, challenging and defeating the Japanese navy there? Such a war involved the Philippines. That was contemplated by the naval war planners in the 1920s and 1930s,

---

* Miller, *War Plan Orange,* p. xix. "In their finest hour, the experts [already in the late 1920s] designed a . . . siege of Japan and calculated the requirements of the long war it would climax, providing for future planners accurate forecasts of the final campaigns of World War II" (p. 133). In early 1933 Captain R. A. Koch of the Naval War College wrote a paper, forwarded to Roosevelt, in which he foresaw a three- or four-year war with Japan, at the end of which the American fleet would be four times larger than the Japanese one (pp. 158–159).

including even a plan for building a large naval base on one of the Philippine islands. "A through ticket to the Philippines" was considered by the planners during the 1920s and early 1930s, but by 1939 and 1940 that idea faded. There were strategists and admirals who thought that in the case of a war with Japan, the Philippines might be indefensible. The second and, in many ways, allied question was whether Japan could be completely defeated by a maritime war. None of the naval war planners, well before the Second World War, contemplated the necessity of an American invasion of Japan.*

Until 1939 Orange meant what could be called a "limited war," a war in the Pacific between two Great Powers but not a world war. But the dramatic tidal wave of what was to be a Second World War changed everything. We have seen that in May and June 1940 Roosevelt ordered a portion of the navy to be moved to the Atlantic when the possibility suddenly arose that Britain would succumb to Germany. A few months later this dreadfully imminent prospect gave way to Britain holding out, of course with increasing American support. That involved strategic moves not only in the Atlantic but also in the Pacific. In September 1940, again in November, and then in January–February 1941, the British invited the American fleet to join them at the great British Far Eastern base of Singapore (whose worth they overestimated until their naval disaster off Malaya in December 1941, losing Singapore two months later). The purpose of the British was to involve the United States more and more on their side in the war, now in the Pacific as well as in the Atlantic, for all kinds of reasons. The chiefs of the American navy — wisely — refused that

---

* In 1935 Captain (the later famous Admiral) William C. Halsey was one of the army officers allotted to the Naval War College, where he said (as he repeated at the Army War College): "In the first place the Navy cannot win a war. The war must be decided on land." Gole, *Road to Rainbow*, p. 39.

Singapore offering. By that time — at the end of 1940 — Orange had given way to Rainbow, indeed to Rainbow Five; and there was a Joint Army and Navy Board, planning the war together.

Until 1940 the class size of the Army War College had been similar to that of the Naval War College.* But there was one great difference. Behind the Naval War College there was a great fleet in being. Within the sight of the Army War College there was only a small army: but of course even before 1940 the army war planners had to project a rapidly growing American army in the case of war. The Army War College planners were more concerned with public opinion than were their navy counterparts. In 1938 the war planners agreed that "a mobilized America could handle almost any war, but to mobilize people and things for a big war would take a year or two",† as indeed it was to happen. As early as 1935 an exercise of the Army War College invoked an eventual war with Germany. That was not much more than a war game, the material of its information having been largely what the planners had read in the better newspapers. In 1937 authors of a study stated that the Germans were "aggressive and apparently determined that by rapid maneuver and open warfare the stalemate of trench warfare of the World War [I] will be prevented." "The Germans would make their main efforts in France" — another accurate assessment. But the army's war plans were still limited, directed as they were to the defense of the United States, in accord with the Monroe Doctrine. Many of the plans now involved the Caribbean, and especially the big bulge

* Approximately eighty officers. "Usually some seventy-nine Army and six Navy and Marine Corps students attended. The Army and Naval War Colleges regularly exchanged graduates to attend the other service's school." Gole, *Road to Rainbow,* p. 19.
† Gole, *Road to Rainbow,* p. 85. In 1940 the college made a study of the "influence of public opinion on the conduct of war" (p. 104).

of Brazil into the Atlantic, where the Western Hemisphere was closest to northern Africa.

Then in 1939 things began to change. President Roosevelt appointed George Catlett Marshall as the army's chief of staff on 1 September 1939, the day Germany invaded Poland and the Second World War began — a historic coincidence. What was not a coincidence (or, if so, a fortunate one) was that Marshall got along and worked very well with General Thomas G. Handy, who had been in charge of the Army War College and its War Plans Division since 1936. Both of them were also instrumental in Roosevelt's choice of Admiral Leahy for his chief of staff. Six weeks later, on 14 October 1939, the first Army and Navy Basic War Plan, drafted in August, was presented to the secretaries of the navy and war, and then to Roosevelt. Drafted by Admiral Harold R. Stark, it bore the code name Rainbow No. 1. Within a year the navy's "Oranges" were replaced by "Rainbows" — suggesting the possibility of a two-front war. Both the army and navy planners, the Joint Army and Navy Board, including Admirals Stark and Leahy, agreed that Germany was the main danger and the possible object of a war; the Atlantic rather than the Pacific.* The army war planners insisted that a war could not be won "primarily by naval action."† "The decision in 1940 to defeat Germany first, already recommended at the college by classes since 1935, provided further rationale for a deliberate and conservative strategy in the Pacific."‡ During the winter of 1939–1940 there were other drafts, some of them unfinished, among them "Rainbow X." Then, on 31 May 1940 (note the date: France collapsing, the British army fleeing homeward from Dunkirk,

---

* Keep in mind that in September 1939 Japan was still neutral, not committed to Germany by an alliance. That would change a year later.
† Miller, *War Plan Orange,* p. 223.
‡ Gole, *Road to Rainbow,* p. 91.

Mussolini's Italy about to enter the war on Hitler's side) Rainbow Four was drafted. It included this somber assessment: "The destruction of the British and French Fleets will afford Germany and Italy naval freedom of action in the Atlantic. The surrender of the main British and French naval units will eventually afford Germany and Italy naval equality or superiority with respect of the United States Fleet." "If the British and French Fleets should go out of action in the near future, before adequate expansion and training of our Regular Army had been accomplished," the National Guard would have to be mobilized. *The date of the loss of the British and French Fleets automatically sets the date of our mobilization.** We have seen that at that time Roosevelt still hoped that the British fleet might come over. Rainbow Four was among the first on the agendas of the new secretaries of the navy and war. They approved it on 13 June. It was signed by the president on 14 August. (Rainbow One, presented to him, had been approved only verbally on 14 October 1939.) "Actual hostilities will be preceded by the occupation by United States forces of key British, French, Dutch and Danish possessions in the Western Hemisphere claimed by Germany and Italy as spoils of war. Establish United States Sovereignty in British, French, Dutch and Danish possessions in the Western Hemisphere." This was printed in capital letters.

But then Churchill and the British held out. Roosevelt was edging the United States closer and closer to Britain. A giant armament program, the mobilization of the United States had begun. Among other measures the Army War College, as such, was absorbed into the War Department, most of its officers appointed to work with the Army General Staff. And now, immediately after the reelection of President Roosevelt, on 12 Novem-

* *U.S. War Plans,* p. 34.

ber 1940 appeared the first and basic draft of Rainbow Five, prepared by Admiral Stark, by way of a long memorandum presented to the secretary of the navy. "You may recall my remarks the evening we discussed War Plans for the Navy. I stated then that if Britain wins decisively against Germany we could win everywhere; but that if she loses the problem confronting us would be very great; and while we might not *lose everywhere,* we might, possibly, *not win anywhere.*"* Stark underlined these words. Then he went on:

> It is my opinion that the British are over-optimistic as to their chances for ultimate success. It is not at all sure that the British Isles can hold out, and it may be that they do not realize the danger that will exist should they lose in other regions.
>
> Should Britain lose the war, the military consequences to the United States would be serious. . . .
>
> Obviously, the British Isles, the "Heart of the Empire," must remain intact.
>
> But even if the British Isles are held, this does not mean that Britain can win the war. To win, she must finally be able to effect the complete, or, at least, the partial collapse of the German Reich. (p. 57)

Stark was not sure that this could be accomplished by bombing and blockades.

> Alone, the British Empire lacks the manpower and the material means to master Germany. Assistance by powerful allies is necessary both with respect to men and with respect to munitions and supplies. . . .

* *U.S. War Plans,* pp. 55–56.

The objective in a limited war against Japan would be the reduction of Japanese offensive power chiefly through economic blockade. . . . I do not believe that [the British and the Dutch] alone could hold the Malay Barrier without direct military assistance from the United States. . . .

Purely naval assistance would not, in my opinion, *assure* final victory for Great Britain. Victory would probably depend upon her ability ultimately to make a land offensive against the Axis powers. For making a successful land offensive, British manpower is insufficient. . . . I believe that the United States, in addition to sending naval assistance, would also need to send large air and land forces to Europe or Africa, or both, and to participate strongly in this land offensive. The naval task of transporting an army abroad would be large. . . .

We might temporarily check Japanese expansion by defeating her in a war in a war in the Far East, but to check her permanently would require that we retain possession of, and militarily develop, an extensive and strategically located Asiatic base area having reasonably secure lines of communication with the United States. Retaining, and adequately developing, an Asiatic base area would mean the reversal of long-standing American policy. (pp. 57, 60, 61, 62)

Stark then sketched four different American strategies, A, B, C, and D. Then came his key argument, or recommendation. He began with what may be called a theoretical question: "Shall we direct our efforts toward an eventual strong offensive in the Atlantic as an ally of the British, and a defensive in the Pacific? . . . The odds seem against our being able under Plan (D) to check Japanese expansion unless we win the war in Europe" (pp. 64, 65).

This was Plan D, or "Plan Dog." It was to become soon Rainbow Five. Stark recommended that American-British staff conversations ensue. They were held in Washington for two months, from 29 January to 27 March 1941. "The broad strategic objective . . . of the Associated Powers will be the defeat of Germany and her Allies" (p. 69).

The British and of course Churchill, were very pleased to accept Rainbow Five. On 22 November, Churchill sent a minute "to First Lord and First Sea Lord" (General Ismay) to see: "In my view Admiral Stark is right, and Plan D is strategically sound, and also most highly adapted to our interests. We should, therefore, so far as opportunity serves, in every way contribute to strengthen the policy of Admiral Stark, and should not use arguments inconsistent with it."*

Churchill tried to have an American navy task force come to Singapore. In vain, because Roosevelt had already allotted much of the navy to the Atlantic. A war against Japan must be necessarily limited. Roosevelt vetoed any large buildup of the fleet in the Pacific.

Germany First . . . *that* was the right decision. It decided much of the war — and much else too. It was so much in accord with the inclinations and ideas of Franklin Roosevelt that many people, including the writer of these lines, thought for a long time that it was Roosevelt who persuaded his admirals and generals to plan and proceed accordingly; but now we know that America's professional war planners and the president not only saw matters largely alike but that the vision and eventually the influence of

*Winston S. Churchill, *The Second World War,* vol. 2, *Their Finest Hour* (Cambridge, 1949), pp. 690–691.

the former preceded the decisions of the latter. In other words: the divisions among the American population (to which I must once more return) proved not to be a definite handicap to their naval and military planners. There were important and intelligent officers who held different views of Germany than had most of their superiors; some of the former had had excellent relations with German officers; some of them were neither Democrats nor New Dealers; not internationalists or interventionists and quite probably not Germany Firsters.* Yet, whatever their personal opinions, they chose not to compromise their loyalty and obedience to their chiefs. And thus the planning and the adoption of Rainbow Five were great examples, illuminating (in the original meaning of that word) the characters and the abilities of well-trained officers in the armed services of the giant American democracy.

◆ ◆ ◆

There remain a few additional considerations beyond the vision and the adoption of Rainbow Five, thirteen months before Pearl Harbor. In one important sense Rainbow Five was more prescient than was the president. As late as 1941, at the very time when the British were suffering yet another defeat in the eastern Mediterranean, and before Hitler invaded Russia, Roosevelt in a letter to Churchill wrote that sea power was the key to history

---

* Examples: Colonel Truman Smith, air attaché in Berlin and a close friend, associate, and supporter of Charles Lindbergh; or Colonel, later General, Albert Wedemeyer, who studied in the Kriegsakademie in Berlin in 1937.

and victory.* Yet that was no longer so — as Hitler, among others, recognized.

The army planners of Rainbow Five knew that. So did the navy. General Eisenhower, later the commander of the Allied forces in Europe, did not like Admirals Stark and King.† Yet these admirals knew that sooner or later an American land offensive in Europe was inevitable.‡ In April 1942, more than two years before the actual invasion of Western European on D-Day, Roosevelt and Marshall ordered the planning of an early landing in Normandy to occur in November 1942, to establish an American bridgehead around Cherbourg. Churchill said that this was premature. He was right: such an early invasion would have been a disaster. He was listened to; his views prevailed, indeed, into 1943, when he convinced Roosevelt and Marshall to continue going into Italy after the Allied conquest of Sicily. Thereafter Churchill's influence declined. By 1944 the contribution of American manpower began to far exceed that of the British. But the main thrust of Rainbow Five, "Germany First," remained unchanged, and rightly so.

American predominance was of course obvious in the Pacific.

* "In the last analysis the Naval control of the Indian Ocean and the Atlantic Ocean will in time win the war." Roosevelt to Churchill, 1 May 1941.
† Gole, *Road to Rainbow,* p. 30.
‡ The original draft of Rainbow Five was officially approved in May and June 1941 by the secretaries of war and the navy. On 9 July, Roosevelt directed the service secretaries to prepare an estimate of requirements for a global war (*U.S. War Plans,* pp. 103 ff.). On 11 September these estimates called for an army of 215 divisions, thirty-two battleships and fourteen aircraft carriers. It also added (ibid., p. 104): "It is out of the question to expect the United States and its Associates to undertake in the near future a sustained and successful land offensive against the center of the German power. . . . [But] the Associated Powers cannot defeat Germany by defensive operations."

The British, suffering one of their worst defeats at Singapore, were unable to defend Australia and New Zealand by themselves. But the priority of Rainbow Five remained unaffected by the coming of the war with Japan. Indeed, to some extent it compromised the readiness for that war. No American warships were sent to the Pacific from the Atlantic until after Pearl Harbor. In late 1941 the Joint Chiefs of Staff decided to fortify and build airfields on the islands of Guam and Wake, well in the western Pacific and beyond the accepted lines of American defenses in its eastern half.* Meanwhile, General MacArthur insisted on getting bombers to the Philippines. (He succeeded, wrongly so.) On 5 November 1941 General Marshall and Admiral Stark told the president that to send forces to China "the services would have to denude the Atlantic and thereby imperil Britain and the Germany-first strategy of Rainbow Five."† As late as 1944 there were plans to send a considerable American army to China. Yet, as the war against Japan went on, it became more and more evident that American forces might have to invade and conquer islands closer and closer to Japan and in the end invade Japan itself. That dreadful necessity had not occurred to the Rainbow Five planners in 1940 and 1941. Fortunately enough, that did not have to happen. Not only because of the atomic bomb, as many believe: but principally because the slogan of Unconditional Surrender was—wisely—modified by President Truman and by some of his advisers. They chose not to insist on the removal of the Emperor Hirohito from the Japanese throne; in other words, Japan's surrender was not entirely "unconditional." It was Hirohito alone who was able to impress upon the Japanese people

---

*It is noteworthy that the often Asia-Firsters of the America First Committee criticized that publicly "as beyond America's legitimate venue of defense." Miller, *War Plan Orange,* p. 242.
† Miller, *War Plan Orange,* p. 318.

that they must cease fighting, that they had lost this war. Much good came from that: or, perhaps better put, much more harm was spared. (Had President Wilson, in October 1918, not insisted on the abolition of monarchy in Germany, the world would have been spared even more harm, including that of Hitler.) But 1945 was, after all, the justification of the foresight of Rainbow Five, as indeed the war against Japan ended not more than three months after the surrender of Germany.

Sixty years after 1941 the excellent historian of *The Road to Rainbow*, Henry G. Gole, wrote: "The degree to which American War College planners were convinced that American material strength ensured absolute victory is striking. That conclusion was not chauvinistic. Events would demonstrate that American material resources would smother Germany and Japan while simultaneously providing masses of material to keep Britain, the Soviet Union, and China in the war."* Yes, but American material strength was not all. Among other things, too much was expected from American air superiority throughout the war.† More important, and commendable, was the confidence and the willingness to the planners of Rainbow Five to help steer the course of the American ship of state against large currents of what was called public opinion or, even more, popular sentiment. Both before and after Pearl Harbor for most Americans warring against Japan was more popular than warring against Germany. But Rainbow Five's priorities were the opposite. For once, the interests of the United States amounted to something higher than popular sentiments. On 3–4 December 1941 the

---

* Gole, *Road to Rainbow*, p. 153.
† In the Victory estimates of November 1941: "Destruction of [the social and economic] structure [of Germany] will virtually break down the capacity of the German nation to wage war" and German morale (*U.S. War Plans*, p. 120). This did not happen.

headlines of the isolationist *Chicago Tribune* blared forth a sensational revelation: the main features of the "Victory Plan," that is of Germany First, that is of Rainbow Five. It did not matter — and not only because four days later the tidal wave of the news of Pearl Harbor submerged all opposition, at least for awhile. Whoever leaked the war plan to the *Chicago Tribune* did not matter. The men who had drafted Rainbow Five were convinced of its rightness — commendably so.

SEVEN

The Second World War and the Origins of the Cold War

Many people, including political "scientists" and historians, have seen and still see the "cold war" as a consequence of World Communism. In the United States leading "conservatives," James Burnham and William Buckley, wrote that in 1917 "history changed gears." In Germany, Ernst Nolte, a historian, wrote that beginning in 1917, with the Communist revolution in Russia, the entire history of the twentieth century thereafter was that of a "European civil war." This is — they are — wrong. The "cold war" was a consequence of the Second World War. Its cause was the nature of the Russian occupation of most of Eastern Europe and of eastern Germany. The words *cold war* came into existence in the United States in 1948. We may pin down the chronological limits of the "war": 1947 to 1989. In 1947 Russian and Communist rule in the eastern portion of Europe became, by and large, unconditional; in 1989 the Communist governments in Eastern Europe ceased to exist. True, the first reactions of the American government against further Communist or Russian expansion and against the aggressiveness of the Russian government began to appear a year before 1947, and the ending of hostility between the American and Russian governments about two years before 1989, and the final end of Communism and the dissolution of the Soviet Union in 1991: still, it is proper and reasonable to fix the frame, the duration of the cold war, from 1947 to 1989. What remain arguable are the related questions: What was the main "cause" of the cold war, Communism? or Russia? or both? And — if the cold war was but a consequence of the Second World War, was that consequence necessarily inevitable?

This book is about the Second World War: and while it may be the expectable temptation of authors to attribute exceptional importance to their subject, about this matter of the origins of the cold war this writer thinks that he must not be accused of special pleading; and he hopes that at least some of his readers will share his sense of indignation about the ideological — that is, Communism-obsessed — explanation of the cold war and even of the Second World War. For those who think and say and write that the history of the twentieth century was governed by the epic struggle of Democracy (or Freedom) against Communism imply that the Second World War was but a secondary chapter, an interruption of the great confrontation with that evil force. But the opposite is true. The history of the twentieth century, worldwide, was marked by the two world wars. The Russian Revolutions of 1917 were a consequence of the First World War, the cold war of the Second. There is no need to argue this again, except to recognize yet another unpleasant tendency, an inclination especially current among American "conservatives," to think and to assert that Communism was more evil than National Socialism. A seemingly (but only seemingly) broader-minded version is the one adopted by so-called liberals, the thesis that the twentieth century represented the struggle between "Democracy" and "Totalitarianism." There is no use to argue about that either, except perhaps to recognize that the minds of some people are broad enough to be flat.

So back to the important question: was the cold war unavoidable at all? Was a postwar clash of interests between Soviet Russia on one side and America and Britain on the other side inevitable? Franklin Roosevelt did not think so. Winston Churchill hoped not — at least for a while. Adolf Hitler was convinced of it.

◆ ◆ ◆

Franklin Roosevelt's decisions and thoughts and inclinations involving Russia and Communism and Stalin have been analyzed and described and categorized for more than sixty years now. According to his harsh critics, his ideas were deluded, illusionary, and shallow; according to his admirers, they were pragmatic, shrewd, and realist. There is truth in both kind of assertions, but perhaps only in the sense of La Rochefoucauld's maxim that there is at least *some* truth even in what your worst enemies say about you. Franklin Roosevelt's character was complex. Regarding Russia and Stalin his mind was not. He was willing to accord them a goodly amount of benevolence. The origins of that are discernible even before June 1941, that is, before Hitler's invasion of Russia. In 1933 it was his decision (long overdue) for the United States to give diplomatic recognition to the Soviet Union, establishing official state relations between these two largest states of the world.* Well before 1933 Roosevelt thought that most of the

---

*This accorded with the views of his wife, whose character and personality were very different from his, affecting their marital relations: yet that was

Republicans' views of the world were isolationist and parochial. Not all of them were: but had a Republican such as Hoover or Taft been president of the United States in 1940, Hitler would have won the war. Roosevelt's decision to stand by Churchill and Britain at the risk of war remains to his enduring credit.

But then in 1941 Stalin and his Russia suddenly became virtual allies of Britain and of the United states. Roosevelt's first reactions to this event were cautious. He was aware of Republican and America Firster and isolationist but also of Catholic sentiments within the American people — so, unlike Churchill, he did not immediately declare an American alliance with the Soviet Union upon the news of its invasion by Hitler. But, like Churchill, Roosevelt welcomed this new turn in the war. Less than two months after the start of the German war in Russia he wrote a message to the pope, Pius XII, suggesting that the Holy See reconsider its categorical condemnation of the Soviets and of their atheistic Communism — a sign or symptom of Roosevelt's thinking as well as of his politic concern with sections of American popular opinions.

But our purpose here is not a narrative survey of American-Russian relations during the Second World War. It is the question whether the clash, or conflict, or struggle between the United States and Russia could have been avoided. Roosevelt thought so. That conflicts between them would occur he knew; but he also thought that they would eventually fade away. And so, before looking at some of these conflicts that were accumulating especially toward the end of the war — whence they may be seen as early symptoms of the coming cold war — we may as well sum up something about this president's general inclinations involv-

---

one of the instances when Eleanor's and Franklin's views of the world were more in accord than were their personalities.

ing the Soviet Union and Stalin. They were threefold (or, in other words, they existed on three connected levels). One was his inclination to believe that he could charm — or, perhaps more precisely: impress and influence — Stalin with the benevolence and amiability of his personal behavior, with his words and manners. (That was an asset that he had often employed in his domestic political relationships with success.) The second was his consequent tendency to distance himself from Churchill, especially when Stalin was present, at times, alas, demonstrably so. (That was a tactic of the politician Roosevelt that we may lament in retrospect: it did no good, and it hurt Churchill, but also suggested that for Roosevelt the American alliance with Russia now was even more important than the alliance with Britain.) The third was Roosevelt's overall view of where and how the history of the world was moving. He saw the United States as somewhere in the middle, in the middle between Stalin and Churchill, or between the Russian and the British empires, but also between the rough pioneer Russian system moving toward an egalitarian future and the British Empire, admirable in some ways, but antiquated and backward. (That was a thorough misreading: for it was Russia, not Britain, that was backward, led by a reincarnation of someone like Ivan the Terrible — whom Churchill saw, not altogether wrongly, as a peasant tsar.) Over all of this was Roosevelt's belief — that, at least for some time, Churchill also hoped at least to some extent — that his wartime alliances would have a lasting effect on Stalin and, consequently, on the international behavior of the Soviet Union.

There *were* some reasons for that hopeful expectation — though, as events would show, not much and not enough.

These reasons rested on Stalin's statesmanship. His ability for that ought not be dismissed easily. During the Second World War Stalin spoke and acted often not at all like a Communist revolutionary but like a Russian statesman. Well before 1939 he realized the advantages — and the inevitability — of seeing the world, and himself, thus.* In this he was way above, and ahead of, his toadies in the Politburo, including Molotov. Anthony Eden recalled to Sumner Welles (a once leading American diplomat) a conversation with Stalin, who said: "Hitler is a genius but he doesn't know when to stop." Eden: "Does anyone know when to stop?" Stalin: "I do."†

Added to this was Stalin's genuine respect for Roosevelt. He knew that Roosevelt had ordered huge shipments of armaments and goods for Russia very soon after the German invasion. In sveral instances during the war he agreed with Roosevelt; on other occasions he deferred to him. Roosevelt took hope and encouragement from Stalin's statement to Churchill's envoy Beaverbrook in October 1941 that the Soviet Union's alliance with the United States and Britain "should be extended."‡ In July 1942 he agreed to Roosevelt's request to divert forty American bombers destined for Russia to the British army badly pressed in western Egypt. In November 1942, in answer to Roosevelt's apologetic explanations about having had to deal with Admiral Darlan, the former Vichyite commander, in North Africa, Stalin wrote that Roosevelt's policy was "perfectly correct."§ In that month

---

* I attempted to describe and emphasize this (including his fatal errors) in my *June 1941: Hitler and Stalin.* On one occasion, in August 1944, Molotov said to Stalin: Germany will try to make peace with Churchill and Roosevelt. Stalin answered: "Right, but Roosevelt and Churchill won't agree."

† Drew Pearson, *Diaries, 1939–1959,* ed. Tyler Abell (New York, 1974), p. 134.

‡ *My Dear Mr. Stalin: The Complete Correspondence of Franklin D. Roosevelt and Joseph V. Stalin,* ed. Susan Butler (New Haven, 2005), p. 62.

§ The — temporary — American "deal" with Darlan, dictated by necessity at that time, was violently criticized by liberals, Leftists, and Communists throughout the world.

Roosevelt's special envoy, General Patrick Hurley, reported to Roosevelt that "Stalin's attitude was uniformly good-natured, his expressions were always clear, direct and concise. His attitude toward you and the United States was always friendly and respectful."* Of course, Stalin knew what Roosevelt wanted to hear; and also what the president wanted from him (for Russia to enter the war against Japan; and the Soviet Union's willingness to enter the United Nations, the first promise made at Teheran, the second at Yalta). Still, Stalin was genuinely shocked by the sudden news of Roosevelt's death on 12 April 1945. He overruled Molotov, ordering him to proceed to Washington and to the United Nations' San Francisco Conference. Next day Soviet newspapers carried the news of Roosevelt's death on their front pages, surrounded by black borders.

At the same time the first serious symptoms of a potential conflict with the Soviet Union already existed. But before describing some of them I must correct the legend, assiduously disseminated by Roosevelt's admirers, that shortly before his

---

*My Dear Mr. Stalin, p. 97. "Respectful": note Stalin's language to Roosevelt on another occasion (2 December 1944) about Russian relations with France: "I ask your advice on this question as well." Ibid., p. 270.

In 1971 Harriman, angered by Dean Acheson's rather self-serving account of himself and Roosevelt and Truman (in an interview in the British journal the *Listener*), spoke to Arthur Schlesinger, Jr., at length, which the latter found important enough to reproduce almost verbatim in his *Journals, 1952–2000* (New York, 2007), pp. 335–336. "FDR was basically right in thinking he could make progress in personal relations with Stalin. My only difference with him was that he was more optimistic about how much progress he could make. Stalin was very much impressed with Roosevelt; you could almost say that he was in awe of Roosevelt. . . . I don't know what would have happened if FDR had lived. I only know that things would not have been the same. . . . Of course Roosevelt had his defects. . . . Sometimes he kept talking because he didn't want to give the other fellow a chance to talk. Sometimes he was overly naive."

death he had begun to change or indeed did change his mind about Stalin, ready to oppose the latter when and if must. Churchill urged him to do so, but in vain. On 11 April 1945, the day before he died, the tired and wan Roosevelt at Warm Springs did dictate an often cited sentence in a message to Churchill: "We must be firm, however, and our course thus far is correct." Yet that was but a throwaway last sentence in a dispatch whose essence was this: "I would minimize the general Soviet problem as much as possible because these problems, in one form or another, seem to arise every day and most of them straighten out." In Moscow, Averell Harriman, Roosevelt's friend and ambassador, had begun, somewhat belatedly, to have serious doubts about the Russians' behavior. That same day, 11 April, Roosevelt dispatched to Harriman his last message to Stalin: "There must not, in any event, be mutual mistrust and minor misunderstandings of this character [they involved Poland] should not arise in the future."* Before sending it on to Stalin, Harriman suggested deletion of the word *minor*. The president's chief of staff Admiral Leahy, working in the Map Room of the White House in Washington, drafted Roosevelt's response early next morning: "I do not wish to delete the word 'minor.'" A few minutes after one o'clock—after Roosevelt had had his lunch—Leahy received Roosevelt's approval of the final text. Nine minutes later the president was struck by "a terrific pain." These were his last words. He died two hours later.

Keep in mind how during the Second World War a few men—Hitler, Churchill, Stalin, Roosevelt—governed the history of the world. This brings us to Winston Churchill. His critics (and even some of his admirers) have written that just as Neville Chamberlain had failed to understand Hitler, Churchill had failed to

* *My Dear Mr. Stalin,* pp. 322–323.

understand Stalin. That parallel will not run. Chamberlain, until September 1939, had his illusions about Hitler and Germany. Churchill had few illusions about Stalin and Russia. He did not think that Stalin was an international revolutionary. We saw some of this in an earlier chapter, attempting to reconstruct the division of Europe developing during the war. Churchill thought that the best way to avoid, or at least limit, coming conflicts with Stalin and Russia was to agree on a more or less precise definition of the geographical extent of Russia's sphere of interest before the end of the war. Because of Roosevelt's opposition Churchill did not have his way. After 1943 his prestige was still great, but his and Britain's power were not. He, too, was tired and worn; he tried to influence the Americans; but in the end he thought it best to defer to them. His wish for a special relationship between Britain and the United States existed throughout his life. It governed, also, the last volume of his *History of the Second World War.* In 1952 he wrote in a confidential letter to Eisenhower that he chose not to recall or emphasize or even mention some of his disagreements with the Americans during the last and decisive year of the war in Europe. (That accorded with his tendency of never reminding people: "I told you so.") But it also obscured essential matters. After all, the title of his sixth volume was *Triumph and Tragedy.* That word *tragedy* did not occur to any American or Russian after the war. The tragedy was the division of Europe, and the coming of a cold war. The astonishing acuity of Churchill's vision was recounted not by himself but by General De Gaulle in his *Memoirs.* In November 1944 De Gaulle, trying to coax Churchill away from the Americans, said that they were shortsighted and inexperienced, allowing vast portions of Eastern Europe to fall to the Russians. Churchill said, yes, that was so. "Russia is now a hungry wolf amidst a flock of sheep. But after the meal comes the digestion period." Russia would not be able to digest all of her Eastern European conquests. That was so — but only in the long run. Before that the cold war arose.

Of that eventuality Adolf Hitler was convinced. Much of his strategy and policy was inspired by what he saw as an irrepressible conflict between the Anglo-Americans and the Russians. Before the end of the war he spoke of this to his confidants on many occasions. He saw, or at least pretended to see, the first signs of such a conflict, even the prospect of a clash of arms, from which he and Germany would profit. But his time was running out. He killed himself on 30 April 1945. Five days before that American and Russian troops met and shook hands in the middle of Germany, near Torgau on the Elbe, a symbolic event of a division of Europe not far from Wittenberg, where more than four hundred years before Luther had made his declaration, whereafter Germany and Christendom became divided.

◆ ◆ ◆

A book summing up the episodes and attempts with which Hitler's regime tried to divide the Allied coalition after 1941 remains to be written. Its author will have a difficult task. There were many such attempts; he will have to distinguish between serious and not-so-serious, subtle and not-so-subtle ones; he will have to comprehend not only the intricacies of the different personnel within the regime of the Third Reich but also something about their Allied counterparts; and he ought to surmise at least some things about Hitler's knowledge of these attempts. In this book I can and must do not much more than a summary sketch (or call it "Suggestions for further research"), subordinated to the question about the origins of the cold war. For Hitler's main purpose — and that of other Germans, understandably so — was not only to cause suspicions and frictions between the British and the

Americans and the Russians but to help bring about actual conflicts between them.

Hitler thought and often said to his subordinates and to people who urged him to seek contact with one or another of his adversaries that such a political move had to be preceded by a resounding German military victory in the field, on one front or another. More than one of his most important military decisions he took with that in mind: the battle of Kursk in July 1943 and the last German offensive in Belgium in December 1944, for example. His rationale for these endeavors exists in the record of his own words. Apart from that he put not much faith in diplomatic or political or other clandestine attempts. Not much: but some. He seldom encouraged such; but he did not always discourage them. His consent to such operations, or moves, was seldom explicit; more often it was implicit, in one way or another. That was the case with the several attempts that Heinrich Himmler made, establishing some contact with the services of the Western Allies in several circumstances and on several occasions. It is ever so often the head of the secret services of a state who, no matter how cruel or brutal his record, knows the prospects of defeat and tries to contravene them: such was the case of Fouché near the end of Napoleon, of Beria after the death of Stalin, and of Heinrich Himmler in 1944 and 1945. His underlings' negotiations with certain Jewish persons in Hungary in 1944, their contact with Americans later in that year, their negotiations with Raoul Wallenberg, again in Hungary, near the end of 1944 were promoted for the main purpose of making trouble among the Allies, and preferably between Americans and Russians. Some of them may have been undertaken behind Hitler's back; but not without Hitler's knowledge; and (until the very last days of the war) not against Hitler's wishes.

The most important of such contacts occurred in Italy in 1944 and 1945. In one instance Hitler preceded Himmler. He ordered that the German evacuation of Rome should take place without any damage to the Eternal City; and he suggested to General Kesselring that he try to establish contacts with American generals before or during the German withdrawal. That did not happen; but more important were the — not at all unconditional — surrender negotiations between the SS General Karl Wolff and mostly American (with some British) representatives in Italy and Switzerland beginning in January 1945 — negotiations that not only Himmler but Hitler knew and allowed, implicitly as well as explicitly at times. Wolff and Himmler could take at least some satisfaction from these protracted negotiations. They certainly rattled and irritated Stalin, leading to a short but bitter exchange of messages between him and Roosevelt in early April 1945.* The contacts began with the help of an Italian middleman, Parilli, who thought that certain Germans "had hoped eventually to fight together with [the Americans] against the Russians." "The thought of dividing the Western Allies from the Russians was the last great hope of the German leadership and ran like a red thread through all of the negotiations." Thus two months before Hitler's suicide American generals and an SS general sat at the same table in Switzerland. (On 15 April, Wolff wrote a letter to Allen Dulles, expressing his condolences on President Roosevelt's death.) The next day, 16 April, Himmler — and Hitler — ordered Wolff (the order was repeated three

---

* The main printed sources of this episode are Max Waibel, *1945: Kapitulation in Norditalien* (Basel, 1981); Klaus-Dietmark Henke, *Die amerikanische Besetzung Deutschlands* (Munich, 1995); Bradley D. Smith and Elena Agarossi, *Operation Sunrise* (New York, 1979); and Allen Dulles, *The Secret Surrender* (New York, 1966), the last one considerably self-serving and insubstantial.

times) to Berlin, where he spent more than ten hours with Himmler and the SS chief Kaltenbrunner before seeing Hitler. Next day (the seventeenth) Hitler received Wolff and, in his way, wished him well in his endeavor. He did tell him to perhaps wait a bit before signing an armistice with the Americans, but he still "saw in [these negotiations] a good instrument to cause dissensions within the anti-Hitler coalition." He said to Wolff that the German armies may be fighting for another two months. "During these two decisive months of the war a break . . . between the Russians and the Anglo-Saxons will come, and whichever of the two sides comes to him, he will gladly ally with them against the other."*

Here we must understand that, at least about these matters, Hitler and his subordinates and the majority of the German people were largely in accord. The German people hoped to be dealt better by the Americans than by the Russians (and also than by the English). That was understandable. They had every reason to think and believe that the Americans would treat them with no sentiments of revenge, with less hatred and savagery than the Russians, whom they feared. That was why during the last three months of the war the German armies retreated faster and fought less determinedly along the Western than on the Eastern Front. There were hundreds of episodes when the German population accepted with some relief the American troops overrunning and occupying. There was, too, an element of opportunism in the expectations of the German population about the Americans. The excellent German historian of the American occupation of

---

*Henke, *Die amerikanische Besetzung Deutschlands,* p. 676; Waibel, *1945,* pp. 28, 31, 106, 107–108; see also Christopher Woods, "A Tale of Two Armistices," in K. G. Robertson, ed., *War, Resistance, and Intelligence: Essays in Honour of M. R. D. Foot* (London, 1999), pp. 1–18, about C. R. D. Mallaby, a British SOE officer in Italy; also my *The Hitler of History,* chapter 5.

Germany Henke noted "the astonishing optimism of the [west German] industrial elite" during the first weeks of the American occupation, asserting "business as usual," making references in favor of Americans (and of course to the savagery of Russians). But also against the British: as early as April 1945 some of the Krupp executives asked the Americans to support them against a British commission due to arrive. One of their leaders said to the Americans: "The British want nothing else but the destruction of German industrial competition." No matter how correctly the British occupiers behaved, Germans expected nothing from them but cold contempt; they saw them (but not the Americans) as rigid and determined enemies.* But that had little or nothing to do with the origins of the cold war.

◆ ◆ ◆

What were the first symptoms of the cold war? While keeping in mind that an early symptom does not necessarily result in a protracted crisis, we ought to consider them, at least cursorily. We must also keep in mind the difference, and the time elapsed, between the diagnosis of a symptom and its treatment — and the ability or the inability (which so often suggests the willingness or the unwillingness) to recognize the meaning of the symptom. About this there was a decisive difference between Roosevelt and Churchill. The American inclination was to get on with and through the war: political problems, including peace settlements, must come later. Churchill thought and wrote — even in his toned-down memoir *Triumph and Tragedy* — that, especially

---

* Archbishop (soon to be Cardinal) von Galen in Münster, from whom the British had expected much because of his occasionally brave anti-Nazi sermons, on the first Sunday after Münster had fallen to the British referred in his sermon to these "foreign soldiers in our midst."

toward the end of a great war, military and political decisions cannot be considered separately: "At the summit they are one." He did not have his way.

There were reasons for that American attitude: the continuing war against Japan and the hope of Russian participation in it; the still existing isolationism among many Americans, wishing to end the war in Europe and to bring Americans home as soon as possible. These explain much of the general American unwillingness to confront problems with Stalin and the Soviet Union before the end of the war in Europe and, indeed, for some time thereafter.

Yet—a perhaps pardonable generalization—whereas in science the rules count, in history exceptions may or may not rule but noticed they must be. There was the overall, and often overwhelming, American inclination to brush problems with Russia under the rug (or indeed not to note them at all); but there *were* some signs of an American concern with the Soviet Union and with its potential projects in Europe as the Russian armies were pouring westward. And here any thoughtful historian must at least try to look at the complex nature of what was "American," including "Washington," that is, "the government." Consider only two very different persons in the Roosevelt government, in 1944 and 1945. One was Henry Morgenthau, the secretary of the treasury, a confidant and country neighbor of Franklin Roosevelt; a man who was constantly exaggerating his importance, asserting his closeness to the president, which was not really so. Yet he had his way, at times in important matters. He was the author and propagator of the Morgenthau Plan, aimed at the permanent demolition of Germany's industrial capacity, reducing Germany to hardly more than agriculture. Roosevelt (and even Churchill) accepted that in September 1944, without paying much attention to it; a few months later Morgenthau's plan was ignored and dropped by the different military and other American policy makers in occupied Germany, but still . . . Another person was Allen Dulles, chief of the secret Office of Strategic Services in Switzerland, whom we met at the instance of his palavers with Wolff, the SS general; but Dulles was involved in other negotiations, too, with other non-Nazi Germans. His principal aim was the very opposite of Morgenthau's proposed treatment of Germany. Dulles was concerned about preventing a destroyed Germany, a perilous vacuum of a state whose leaders would be predominantly pro-Russian. He had at least some reasons to be concerned about that: Stalin had already permitted the formation of a committee of German nationalist generals, a possible nucleus of a postwar German regime. It is not clear why Roosevelt chose Dulles to be his — less and less clandestine — representative in Switzerland: but there Dulles was and remained.* Meanwhile, there were a few signs of Roosevelt's concern with Western Europe. His dislike of De Gaulle was connected with the American concern over undue Communist influences in a liberated France, whereto all kinds of clandestine American intelligence agents were sent in August and September 1944. On one occasion (at or before Teheran) Roosevelt sketched the — impractical — design of a narrow American corridor leading to a Russian-occupied Berlin; but that was before the tripartite dis-

---

* Morgenthau's and Dulles's subsequent careers are telling. In July 1945 President Truman got rid of Morgenthau, who presumed to be important enough to be one of Truman's advisers at the coming Potsdam summit conference. Dulles (whose brother John Foster was close to "America First" in 1940, and was a committed Republican, eventually becoming Eisenhower's secretary of state in 1952) became the head of the mighty Central Intelligence Agency, successor of the Office of Strategic Services. It may be said, without much exaggeration, that the Dulles brothers charted the course of the American ship of state during most of the 1950s.

cussions and agreements about the zoning of Germany came about in 1944.

In any event — it was not simply Roosevelt's unwillingness to disagree with Stalin that ultimately led to a rigid division of Europe and to the cold war. A — connected — factor was Roosevelt's lack of interest in Eastern Europe. That was why he was satisfied at Yalta with the imprecise and generally meaningless Declaration of Liberated Europe to which Stalin there agreed (Molotov was seen mumbling to Stalin, warning against its phrasing). That was why Roosevelt, contrary to Churchill, did not want to argue or to even make an issue about Poland with Stalin. There were, too, signs in the United States, mutterings by Republicans and a few congressmen as early as 1944, concerned about the demolition of Germany to the ultimate advantage of Russia. These rumblings were not yet influential; but they were noticed by intelligent foreign observers.*

Churchill was more concerned with Eastern Europe than was Roosevelt — and not only because he felt that Britain owed something to a heroic and tragic Poland. He knew the history and the geography of Europe: he was concerned with Austria, Hungary, Czechoslovakia, rather than with Rumania and Bulgaria: the last two had been often dependent on imperial Russia, while the others belonged to Central, rather than Eastern, Europe (as late as December 1944 he wrote to Roosevelt about that distinction). But his powers were limited — not only in regard to Roosevelt but in regard to Stalin, too: because of their Percentages Agreement that Stalin, especially about Greece, fulfilled exactly. When in December 1944 Churchill sent British troops to Athens to help crush a Communist uprising there, Stalin kept to their agreement

---

* For example, by the Polish ambassador to Washington, the excellent Jan Ciechanowski (see his *Defeat in Victory* [New York, 1947]).

and did nothing.* At the same time the State Department and the American press assailed Churchill's intervention in Greece.

Much of this would change after Yalta. But before that we must look at what were early symptoms of Russian hostility and of Russian suspicions of their Western allies even before that. There were of course many of them. Until D-Day Stalin was both vexed with and suspicious of the slow progress of the Anglo-Americans toward opening up a real Second Front in Western Europe. He feared that Churchill did not want a great invasion of France at all (he had at least some reasons for his suspicions). He was irritated by not having been informed about the American negotiations with Italians before Italy's surrender in 1943, and thereafter by some of the difficulties in transferring Italian warships that had been promised to the Soviet Union. In 1942 and 1943 Roosevelt and Churchill had to consider the danger of a separate peace or armistice between Stalin and Hitler. Stalin did not much fear the converse; but in January 1944 *Pravda* suddenly published an article about some British and German personalities meeting in Madrid about a separate peace. That was entirely untrue; Churchill protested to Stalin. All of this occurred before Yalta.

Was Stalin preparing for an unavoidable conflict with the Capitalist Powers as early as 1944? We cannot tell. What we must keep in mind is a characteristic in Russian history that prevailed under such different regimes as those of Alexander I and Alexander III and then of Stalin in the 1930s and during most of the war: the discrepancy between Russia's foreign policy and its in-

---

* Indeed, the Russian representative in the Allied Control Commission in Athens was instructed to refrain from meeting the Greek Communists. Meanwhile, as during the Darlan episode, American (and also British) liberals, Leftists, and Communists excoriated the British for their "imperialist interventions."

ternal regime. Stalin's alliance with Britain and the United States, his acceptance and occasional cultivation of amicable relations with Churchill and Roosevelt had hardly any consequences and no counterpart in the functioning of the Soviet police state. There there were a few, not insignificant, changes during the war: the promotion of historic symbols and names, a new national anthem, dissolution of the Comintern, open support of the Russian Orthodox Church, and so on: but these were symptoms of nationalism, not of internationalism. When George Kennan, the profoundest American student of Russia, was again posted to Moscow in 1944, he took up his pen and wrote an essay: "Russia — Seven Years Later." It was an extraordinarily perceptive analysis of what could be expected of Russia and of its foreign policy — in many ways it was a forerunner of Kennan's famous "X" article three years later — but an important part of it was Kennan's argument that the essence of the Russian police state remained the same. His essay was not read by many in Washington at that time.

Here we arrive at Yalta — at its relationship to the origins of the cold war. More than sixty years later we have a mass of books and articles and public speeches arguing that Yalta was a failure, or that it was not; again, there is some truth in both kinds of allegations. The euphoria (especially in the United States) that followed the Yalta agreements and declarations was unwarranted; yet Franklin Roosevelt had at least some reasons to think that his meeting of minds with Stalin was a great success. Stalin agreed that the Soviet Union would become part of the United Nations. He promised that Russia would enter the war against Japan three months after the end of the war with Germany. Churchill was not optimistic. His estimation of the value of a future United Nations was much lower than Roosevelt's. He still cared much about Poland — but Poland at the time of Yalta had been overrun and "liberated" by the Soviet armies. The main problem involved no longer the shape, the frontiers of a new postwar Poland; it was the composition and the character of its government, that is, the very nature of its people's lives. In the lengthy discussions about Poland, Stalin was largely adamant, Roosevelt largely bored. A kind of agreement was made, giving some leeway to a British and American presence of observation and interest in free elections due to Poland soon. There was, too, that Declaration of Liberated Europe, general and insubstantial, which Stalin interpreted in his way.

He recognized the Americans' general lack of interest in Eastern Europe. He also recognized their general interest in Western Europe. The future of Germany was a different question: that remained a subject of discussions. Like Roosevelt, Stalin was not disappointed with what happened at Yalta. We may even question whether he foresaw the coming of a great conflict with the United States at that time. Yet soon after Yalta the first symptoms of that began to appear.

◆ ◆ ◆

The British and the Americans soon found that there would be nothing even remotely like free elections in Poland. Stalin was irritated: on 9 April he wrote to Roosevelt that "matters in the Polish question have really reached a dead end" and offered a few insignificant concessions. He tried to inspire some trouble between Roosevelt and Churchill. In his harsh protest against the Bern negotiations with Wolff he wrote (on 3 April) to Roosevelt: "It is known that the initiative in this whole affair belonged to the British," which was not the case. He was suspicious — indeed, more than suspicious: concerned and outraged — that the Germans were surrendering in droves on the Western Front, giving up large cities "without resistance," whereas in the east, in Czechoslovakia, "they were fighting savagely . . . for some unknown [railway] junction which they need as much as a dead man needs a poultice." He was still worried about some kind of a Western deal with Germans.* When three weeks later Churchill refused Himmler's offer to capitulate only in the West, Stalin was relieved and sent an unusually effusive message of appreciation to Churchill.

The theme of this book is not the cold war but the Second World War: not something that began in 1947 but what happened before and during 1945. Yes: ominous symptoms were beginning to accumulate. Many books and articles exist about them. I shall but list them, necessarily briefly. Only a few days after V-E Day, the total German surrender, there was the imminent prospect of an armed clash between British and Commonwealth units and Tito's Communist troops attempting to break into Trieste. (Stalin warned Tito not to provoke the Western Allies there: "What is ours is ours; what is theirs is theirs.") A few weeks earlier an article was printed in a French Communist publication from the pen of a French Communist leader, Jacques Duclos, attacking the head of the Communist Party of the United States, who during the war had instructed his party to support Roosevelt. (The significance of this article has been often exaggerated: Stalin cared not much for Duclos and his ilk.) More important, the FBI and other American secret services now had evidence that efforts were being made by Soviet agents (and especially by American Communist volunteers) to learn more and more about the making of America's secret weapon, the atomic bomb. In January 1945 Stalin and Molotov asked Washington to consider a loan of six billion dollars to a war-ravaged Russia after the end of the war: somehow this

---

* Seven years later, and one year before his death, in March 1952, Stalin suddenly offered something like a "neutral" and united Germany—for the purpose of preventing what he feared: an American-German alliance.

request disappeared in the bureaucratic maze of Washington (though not necessarily because of American ill will). In May and June, before the American armies in central Germany began to withdraw to the zonal boundaries agreed upon, American agents began to corral German scientists and technicians (including Wernher von Braun) in order to bring them to the United States (in some cases for the purpose of employing them in the still continuing war against Japan). After the promised Russian declaration of war against Japan and the Russian invasion against the Japanese forces on the Asian mainland had begun and Japan had surrendered, Stalin asked President Truman to allot to the Soviet Union an occupation zone, one of the four mother islands of Japan. The president of the United States refused, and Stalin had to relent.

Harry Truman's character and his view of the world were different from Franklin Roosevelt's. Yet it must not be thought that his sudden assumption of the presidency meant an instant change in America's relations with Russia—or indeed in the course of the gigantic American ship of state. True, when, less than ten days after he had become President Truman received Molotov in the White House, he spoke to this Russian in strong words to which the latter said that he was thoroughly unaccustomed, but Truman's advisers instantly thought that the president's language was too harsh; and next day Truman thought it better not to press the issue (again it was mostly Poland) with Molotov. When Churchill, a few days after the German surrender, implored Truman to take a harder line with Moscow (it was in that letter that Churchill first used the phrase *iron curtain*), Truman did not follow Churchill's urgings; another few days later he sent Joseph Davies and then Harry Hopkins to Moscow to try to iron out problems with Stalin. During the Potsdam summit meeting in July, Truman's behavior and his impressions of Stalin were still cordial and positive. Throughout 1945 (and even for two years thereafter) Truman did not altogether abandon the hope of maintaining at least acceptable relations with the Soviet Union, and particularly with Stalin.

However: he had — commendably — few or no illusions about Stalin or about Russian ambitions or about Communism. Next year, 1946, was marked by more and more troubles with Russians and Communists, involving Iran, Turkey, Greece, Yugoslavia, Berlin. In March 1946 Truman accompanied Churchill to Fulton, Missouri, where Churchill delivered his famous Iron Curtain speech (though the president and the State Department were careful to state publicly that they were not necessarily associating themselves with the former prime minister's views). By early 1947 Truman's decision was made: to oppose further Soviet advances and aggressions, to contain the Soviet Union and Communism. By that time Stalin had decided to proceed to the more or less full Communization of the countries that had fallen into his sphere of interest in Eastern Europe. There was, as yet, no sharp conflict between the Soviet Union and the United States in China or in the Pacific. Stalin was not sure that Mao Tse-tung and his Communists could win the entire civil war in China. The Soviet Union maintained its embassy in Chungking (Chiang Kai-shek's capital) till the very end (1949). The Soviet Union did not object to the official establishment of the United States' possession or protectorate over the former Japanese islands in Micronesia (1947). But the division of Europe was about complete, and thus the cold war began.

◆ ◆ ◆

So let me conclude this chapter and this book with this last of its six questions: was the cold war inevitable? One occasionally still hears a speculation: had Franklin Roosevelt lived would the cold war have been avoided? *That* question is senseless, because all "what if?" speculations must depend on their plausibility—and by early 1945 Roosevelt was near the threshold of his death. He and people around him did not see, or did not wish to see, that; we know it not only because of what actually happened but from the president's medical records. On another level: had he lived. Franklin Roosevelt was politician enough to know that his protracted insistence on a cordial relationship with Stalin must not be pursued to such extent that his popularity at home would dangerously erode. He might have exacted a few concessions from Stalin, but nothing like a considerable reduction of Russia's control of Eastern Europe (and of eastern Germany).

In late 1945 slowly, gradually, American popular sentiment, and even some segments of American public opinion, were turning against Communism and the Soviet Union, mostly consequent to the news of what Communists and Russians were doing and how they were behaving in Eastern Europe. Still, public opinion and popular sentiments were not identical. Throughout 1945 most of the public and published opinions of journalists and commentators and public personalities remained optimistic and pro-Russian, often exceedingly so. At the same time there were symptoms of increasing popular grumbling against Communism and Communists, even more than with Russia and Russians. Most of that sentiment was still inchoate, mixed up with an isolationism that had been temporarily submerged during the war. But it existed, and it was gaining strength after the end of the war. Its main ingredient was anti-Communism.* When in early

---

*In 1946 the Republican Party made large gains in the congressional elections. Its slogan in the campaign—"Had Enough?"—was more than clever. It suggested: enough of the New Deal, enough of Rooseveltism, enough of liberal illusions and of Communistic influences, enough of all of the propaganda during the Second World War. Etc.

1947 the Truman administration took the first decisive steps toward confronting Russia, an American commitment to stand by and defend Greece and Turkey, the then assistant secretary of state Dean Acheson chose to present this to Congress by drawing a greatly exaggerated and inaccurate prospect of Communism and Communists spreading all over Europe.

And here, compelled as we are to deal at least with the origins of the cold war, about which perhaps more than one hundred books have been written during the past sixty years, we need to cast a look at their two main interpretations. One of them, appearing and widespread in the 1960s, is that the American reaction to Russia in 1945 and after was too rapid and too radical. This interpretation of history, produced by historians and others mostly during the Vietnam War, projected — not very honestly — the dissatisfactions of the 1960s to what had happened twenty years before: wrongly so. The other interpretation, current mostly after the collapse of the Soviet Union, and dependent largely on the revelations of Russian and Communist intelligence machinations in and after 1945, states that the American government's reactions to the Soviet Union's deceptions and aggressiveness was just and taken at the right time. Of these two different interpretations this second is much closer to the truth: but not quite. There is — or ought to be — a third version, reaching necessarily back to 1944 and 1945. This is that the American concern with Russia came not too early but too late; that Stalin should have been confronted with precise and practical questions about the actual limits of his postwar sphere of interest, including the political status of at least some of the countries overrun by the Russian armies, sooner rather than later, in 1944 or early 1945 but certainly before the end of the Second World War in Europe.

Such an interpretation was mentioned by this author in some of his books. Much more important is that such a desideratum was advanced by personages such as Churchill and George Kennan. The former's views were mentioned in this chapter and book earlier; but I must turn, briefly, to Kennan, whose "X" article in 1947 laid down the principles of "containment," often designated as the substance of the architecture of American policy during the cold war. Six years earlier, in 1941, Kennan was an officer in the American embassy in Berlin. After the German invasion of the Soviet Union he wrote a private letter to his friend Loy Henderson in Washington, the gist of which was: "Never—neither then nor at any later date—did I consider the Soviet Union a fit ally or associate, actual or potential, for [the United States]." At the same time he thought that the Russians should be given the material and military support they needed. One may question whether such a combination of military assistance with political aloofness could have been practical or reasonable at all. But one should not question the reasonableness and the foresight of Kennan's views when he was posted to Russia in 1944, especially after the Allies' invasion of Western Europe. Now the problem was "what would be the political outcome of further advances of the Red Army into the remainder of Europe."* It took another year before Kennan's voice was beginning to be heard; first by his ambassador Harriman; then in February 1946 Kennan wrote his now famous Long Telegram; then he was called back to Washington, where he became the director of a Foreign Policy Planning Staff; then in July 1947 came his "X" article with the celebrated word *Containment*. This article, which made him famous: yet its essence was perhaps a restatement of

---

* "The Warsaw Uprising [in August 1944] was, I thought, the point at which, if we had never done so before, we should have insisted on a thoroughgoing exploration of Soviet intentions with regard to the future of the remainder of Europe." *George F. Kennen and the Origins of Containment, 1944–1946: The Kennan-Lukacs Correspondence* (Columbia, Mo., 1997), p. 31.

what has become obvious: the Russians have Eastern Europe now, and we must let them and the world know that they cannot go further. It sometimes happens that an author is best known for a piece of writing that he himself does not see as his best. But here we must go a little beyond that. Soon after 1947 Kennan (as well as Churchill) turned against those who thought and spoke as if Stalin's and Russia's ambitions were endless and the division of Europe unnegotiable and unchangeable. Their arguments were dismissed as illusory—by many of the same men who in 1945 had thought and said that to Churchill's and to Kennan's warnings about Russia attention must not be paid.

That is another story. So let me return to the main question, which perhaps ought to be rephrased: for behind (and within) the question whether the cold war was inevitable there is another question: was Stalin insatiable? Yes and no. So far as his rule over his own people and over his acquired domains went, yes; but so far as the rest of the world, and particularly Western Europe, went, probably no. There is no evidence that either in 1945 or after he aimed or even wished to have the Red Army march farther into Europe, or to establish Communist regimes in Western Europe, or even in Western Germany. This was not so only because he was statesman enough to be cautious. It was so, too, because of his knowledge of the weakness of international Communism. That was the reason of the "iron curtain," the increasingly rigid separation of Eastern Europe from the West. Had he agreed to (as some in the State Department hoped as late as in 1946) an interpretation of the Yalta Declaration of Liberated Europe and of his sphere of interest to allow the presence of governments in Eastern Europe that would be categorically and necessarily pro-Russian but not necessarily Communist,* there

* As he allowed in one, only one, instance: that of Finland.

might not have been much, or any, of a cold war. We may even speculate that if something like that had occurred, Russia could have been a recipient of American generosity, perhaps even of a super–Marshall Plan. But could Stalin agree to something like that?* No — he was not that kind of a man. No: but not because of his Marxist or Communist or ideological extremism, as so many still believe and say and write. He knew that sooner or later a non-Communist Poland or Czechoslovakia or Hungary, no matter how carefully their governments stayed and kept within their categorical requirements of a pro-Russian policy, would be gradually growing closer to the West, connected by a thousand small threads, some more important than others. It was safer, and to him better, to impose on these people rulers who were totally subservient to and dependent on Russia — and to close them off from the rest of Western Europe, no matter how Americans and others might protest.

That was how the cold war began. The Russians swallowed up Eastern Europe; then it went on for forty years during which they had serious instances of digesting some of it (as Churchill had foretold)†; and it ended with their disgorging just about all of it. But one of the results of the cold war was the American national and popular obsession with the evils of Communism that became the principal element in American politics with long-lasting effects. What may belong here is at least a suggestion that the cold war between America and Russia might also have been — at least in one important way — due to a reciprocal misunderstanding. Americans believed, and feared, that, having established Com-

---

* Churchill in 1950: the Soviets fear our friendship even more than they fear our enmity.

† In 1944 to De Gaulle (see pages 169–170); on New Year's Eve in 1952 to his secretary John Colville: by the 1980s "Eastern Europe [would be] assuredly free of Communism."

munism in Eastern Europe, Stalin was now ready to promote, and wherever possible, impose Communism in Western Europe, which was not really the case. Stalin, who knew and understood the weak appeal of Communism beyond the Soviet Union, and who was anxious about America's overwhelming power in and after 1945, thought that the Americans were becoming ready to challenge and upset his rule over Eastern Europe, which also was not the case. The odd thing is that in Europe the turning point of the cold war came in 1956, at the time of the Hungarian Revolution, which stunned and shocked the Russian leadership; but it also gave them a recognition of relief: the Americans were not ready or willing to really challenge or even attempt to alter the division of Europe. That this turning point of American-Russian relations in Europe coincided with a peak of — understandably, because of the brutal Russian suppression of Hungary — American popular hostility for Communism and Russia is, again, another instance of the irony of history (or, perhaps, of the melancholy history of what goes under the imprecise name of "public opinion"). After 1956 in Europe the enmity of the two Superpowers was gradually winding down, until the political division of Europe and of Germany ended with the withdrawal of the Russian empire in 1989 — and the end of the cold war meant also the end of an entire historical century, of the twentieth, dominated by the effects and the results of two world wars.

◆ ◆ ◆

Allow me to append a coda to these considerations.

History does not repeat itself: but there was a geographic similarity to the once strategy of the British and thereafter of the American empires. During four centuries England went to war when a single state threatened to rule Europe, and particularly western European lands, across the English Channel. In the First and the Second World Wars and the cold war, across the Atlantic American statesmanship saw the keeping of Britain and of Western Europe safe from German and then from the prospect of Russian domination as prime and essential American interests. During and after the Second World War this convergence of American and British and Western European interests reached their peak.

More than strategic considerations were involved here. For more than a century and a half after 1776 America moved westward, away from Europe. This was not only a geographic and demographic and strategic direction. It corresponded to the American national and popular belief of the New World's destiny being the opposite of the Old's: *Novus Ordo Seclorum.* In 1917 came a great change: for the first time a large American army crossed the Atlantic from west to east, to help decide a great European war. Soon after that the majority of the American people repudiated that expedition. Yet that repudiation was not entire. During the 1920s the commercial, the intellectual, the cultural ties between the United States and Europe were not diminishing: they were extending. Then came the Second World War, and the apparent ending of American isolationism.

In December 1945 Professor Carlton Hayes, a great American scholar and eminent historian of modern Europe, gave a remarkable presidential address at the convention of the American Historical Association. He said that Frederick Jackson Turner's famous frontier thesis, according to which the history and the destiny and the very essence of the American people were determined by a constant and uninterrupted movement westward, thus away from the East Coast, the Atlantic, and Europe, was mistaken. The Second World War itself demonstrated how the destinies, indeed, how the civilizations and the cultures of United States and Western Europe were complementary, because they belonged together. He was right; and so it seemed not only during the Second World War but at least during the first phase of the cold war, when not only strategists and statesmen but many cultured and liberally educated Americans welcomed the end of a protracted isolationism together with such things as a North Atlantic Treaty Organization, an American peacetime commitment to an American presence and a military and political connection with at least Western Europe.

Rightly so . . . but that was nearly sixty years ago. Now, at the time of this writing, there are, lo and behold, entire Eastern European states within NATO, and there is an American military presence in such formerly unimaginable places as Rumania, Macedonia, Caucasian Georgia. At the same time . . . one may ask whether America and Europe are not growing apart? What is not questionable is that the weight of the United States has been shifting westward and southward; and so has the composition of its population — at the beginning of a new age, well after anything like the Second World War.

Acknowledgments

It is not only proper but pleasant to record my sincere indebtedness to the Earhart Foundation, which assisted, among other things, my travels and research in Munich; to Steven Breedlove of the La Salle University Library, always instantly helpful when I tell him that I need items of unusual publications for my sources; to Dr. Helmut Rechenberg in Munich; and especially to Professors Evan Bukey and Klaus Fischer, who read my manuscript with especial care, and whose comments, as so often, illuminated my mind.

A Dutch translation of this book, identical with the English-language edition, except for Chapter 1, was published in October 2008 under the title *Lands kromme lijnen: Zes resterende vragen oven de tweede wereloorlog* (Amsterdam: Mets and Schilt).

Pickering Close
Phoenixville, Pennsylvania
2004–2008

Index